OXFORD WORLD'S CLASSICS

GORGIAS

PLATO (c.427–347 BC), Athenian philosopher-dramatist, has had a profound and lasting influence upon Western intellectual tradition. Born into a wealthy and prominent family, he grew up during the conflict between Athens and the Peloponnesian states which engulfed the Greek world from 431 to 404 BC. Following its turbulent aftermath, he was deeply affected by the condemnation and execution of his revered master Socrates (469–399) on charges of irreligion and corrupting the young. In revulsion from political activity, Plato devoted his life to the pursuit of philosophy and to composing memoirs of Socratic enquiry cast in dialogue form. He was strongly influenced by the Pythagorean thinkers of southern Italy and Sicily, which he is said to have visited when he was about 40. Some time after returning to Athens, he founded the Academy, an early ancestor of the modern university, devoted to philosophical and mathematical enquiry, and to the education of future rulers or 'philosopher-kings'. The Academy's most celebrated member was the young Aristotle (384–322), who studied there for the last twenty years of Plato's life. Their works mark the highest peak of philosophical achievement in antiquity, and both continue to rank among the greatest philosophers of all time.

Plato is the earliest Western philosopher from whose output complete works have been preserved. At least twenty-five of his dialogues are extant, ranging from fewer than twenty to more than three hundred pages in length. For their combination of dramatic realism, poetic beauty, intellectual vitality, and emotional power they are unique in Western literature.

ROBIN WATERFIELD was born in 1952. After graduating from Manchester University, he went on to research ancient Greek philosophy at King's College, Cambridge. He has been a university lecturer (at Newcastle upon Tyne and St Andrews), and an editor and publisher. Currently, however, he is a self-employed consultant editor and writer, whose books range from philosophy to children's fiction. He has also translated works by Aristotle, Plato, Plutarch, and Xenophon, including, for Oxford World's Classics, Plato's *Republic* and *Symposium*, Aristotle's *Physics*, and Herodotus, *The Histories*.

OXFORD WORLD'S CLASSICS

*For over 100 years Oxford World's Classics have brought
readers closer to the world's great literature. Now with over 700
titles—from the 4,000-year-old myths of Mesopotamia to the
twentieth century's greatest novels—the series makes available
lesser-known as well as celebrated writing.*

*The pocket-sized hardbacks of the early years contained
introductions by Virginia Woolf, T. S. Eliot, Graham Greene,
and other literary figures which enriched the experience of reading.
Today the series is recognized for its fine scholarship and
reliability in texts that span world literature, drama and poetry,
religion, philosophy and politics. Each edition includes perceptive
commentary and essential background information to meet the
changing needs of readers.*

OXFORD WORLD'S CLASSICS

PLATO

Gorgias

Translated with an Introduction and Notes by
ROBIN WATERFIELD

OXFORD
UNIVERSITY PRESS

OXFORD
UNIVERSITY PRESS

Great Clarendon Street, Oxford OX2 6DP

Oxford University Press is a department of the University of Oxford.
It furthers the University's objective of excellence in research, scholarship,
and education by publishing worldwide in

Oxford New York

Athens Auckland Bangkok Bogotá Buenos Aires Calcutta
Cape Town Chennai Dar es Salaam Delhi Florence Hong Kong Istanbul
Karachi Kuala Lumpur Madrid Melbourne Mexico City Mumbai
Nairobi Paris São Paulo Singapore Taipei Tokyo Toronto Warsaw

with associated companies in Berlin Ibadan

Oxford is a registered trade mark of Oxford University Press
in the UK and in certain other countries

Published in the United States
by Oxford University Press Inc., New York

First published as a World's Classics paperback 1994
Reissued as an Oxford World's Classics paperback 1998
Reissued 2008

British Library Cataloguing in Publication Data

Data available

Library of Congress Cataloging in Publication Data

Plato.
[Gorgias. English]
Gorgias / Plato; translated by Robin Waterfield.
p.   cm.—(Oxford world's classics)
Includes bibliographical references and indexes.
1. Ethics—Early works to 1800.   2. Political science—Early works
to 1800.   I. Waterfield, Robin, 1952– .   II. Title.   III. Series.
B371.A5W37   1994   170—dc20   93–48984

ISBN 978-0-19-954032-7

9

Printed in Great Britain by
Clays Ltd, St Ives plc

For Julian

CONTENTS

INTRODUCTION

SHORTLY after the beginning of *Gorgias*, the dialogue is announced to be an enquiry into rhetoric. In ancient Athens of the fifth and fourth centuries BC rhetoric was an essential political tool. For most of this period, Athens was a radical democracy. Every male citizen from the city itself and its outlying districts had the right to attend the Assembly and take part in the decision-making process by voicing his approval or disapproval of a motion. Motions were proposed and countered in speeches. The ability to speak well in front of the Athenian people was important, then. Particular motions and political careers were made or broken by a speaker's ability.

Two and a half thousand years later, why on earth should one wish to read a book about an adjunct of a defunct political system, even when it was written by one of the acknowledged geniuses of Western literature and thought? Rhetoric hardly touches our lives now, it seems; apart from the rare occasions when we might attend a rally of some kind, it is something that happens remotely, in our own governmental assemblies or on our TV screens. There is little we can do about it, even if we are won over by a persuasive speaker. The importance of rhetoric seems to have receded.

Plato would be the first to argue that the impression that rhetoric has receded from our lives is incorrect. At 463a ff. he has Socrates describe rhetoric as a kind of flattery and claim that all kinds of flattery are good at taking on different guises. Even if the importance of rhetoric for political purposes has receded these days, rhetoric remains a strong presence in our lives in other guises. We are still constantly bombarded by people trying to persuade us. The media are full of apparently convincing presentations of products and points of view. And they work. Countless surveys have shown that faced in a shop with a choice between a product whose name is known through advertising and an unfamiliar one, we invariably choose the one which advertising has persuaded us is nutritious or effective or good value or whatever. And everyone knows the experience of reading a newspaper or listening to the radio or watching TV or even talking with friends, and finding an argument plausible—until you come across a convincing presentation of an alternative point of view on the same issue, and become persuaded by that one instead. In short, then, political systems may have changed drastically since ancient Athenian times, but human nature has not changed that much. We can still have superficial knowledge or deep knowledge of an issue. We can still be swayed if we have only superficial knowledge—and even by people who know as little as ourselves, if they can speak well and have a plausible technique.

Of course, it is only possible to be swayed like this one way and another if one is not in full possession of the facts. If I am an expert dietitian, I am unlikely to choose product X over product Y, even if product X has been extensively advertised, if I know from my expertise that product Y is better for me. And if I have thought about and looked into an issue, I have probably formed a position on it, and am less likely to be convinced by alternative positions, especially when I can see that they are being argued by people who are not in possession of the facts. Surely it is self-evident that I should be guided by expert knowledge, rather than by specious beliefs. How can I learn to see through specious arguments? Would an expert recommend different beliefs and activities from those the admen and rhetoricians recommend or assume? The rhetorician promises to teach me how to be successful, but how really should one measure success—by worldly achievements or what?

These are the crucial issues for Plato, and this is why *Gorgias* is still worth reading. The book is not a treatise on rhetoric, but an investigation (as Plato's earlier dialogues invariably are) into human nature and ways of life. It is about our inner life, as much as our outer, political life. The dialogue falls neatly into three stages, depending on whether Gorgias, Polus, or Callicles is arguing with Socrates, who was Plato's mentor and is the ever-present hero of the early dialogues. A summary of these stages will show how Plato takes the seemingly impersonal topic of rhetoric and uses it to raise questions of urgent personal importance—timeless questions, as relevant today as in fifth-century Athens.

The personal and moral tone of *Gorgias* is typical of the early Platonic dialogues (often called simply the Socratic dialogues), of which our dialogue is a kind of culmination (whatever the precise date of its composition—see the note on 470d), in the sense that it addresses issues at the very heart of Socratic philosophy. In another early dialogue, one of the characters tells another: 'You don't seem to appreciate what happens when you come into close proximity with Socrates and strike up a conversation with him. Whatever the original topic of your conversation is, before long he's bound to head you off and finally trap you into trying to explain your own way of life and how you've lived up to now' (*Laches* 187e). This is why Socrates frequently demands of his interlocutors—as he does at *Gorgias* 500b (see also the comparable demands for sincerity at 475d–476a, 494c–d, and 495a–b)—that they voice only their genuine beliefs. We live by our beliefs, so if they accede to this demand, they are laying their lives on the line; and if their beliefs change (as a result of Socratic questioning or for whatever reason), the way they live will change.

Socrates begins, then, by talking to the famous rhetorician Gorgias (from Leontini in Sicily) and quizzing him about his area of expertise, rhetoric. 'Area of expertise' translates the Greek word *tekhnē*. Plato draws on assumptions or inferences about what constitutes a *tekhnē* often in the early dialogues. He might assume, for instance, that someone with a *tekhnē* (an expert or professional) can point to his own teacher or teachers, and can teach others—that is, that the *tekhnē* is transmissible and rationally explicable. And he might assume that a *tekhnē* has a product, as the product of shoe-making is shoes, and that each *tekhnē* has only one product or product-area.

So Socrates questions Gorgias by asking him, in effect, what the product of rhetoric is (449d). As is typical in the Socratic dialogues, Gorgias' first answers have to be narrowed down, until his eventual answer is (454e–455a): 'Rhetoric is an agent of the kind of persuasion which is designed to produce conviction, but not to educate people, about matters of right and wrong.'

From there, Socrates proceeds to tie Gorgias up into logical knots, but we already have enough for our purposes. The contrast between conviction and education shows Plato's point: rhetoric is superficial. It relies on persuasive ploys (459d) rather than on expert knowledge of the issues it is addressing. Apart from the area in which Gorgias claims it practises—right and wrong—'advertising' could easily be substituted for 'rhetoric' in the definition. And the self-contradiction by which Socrates refutes Gorgias is also paralleled today. Like a modern adman, Gorgias claims that his techniques for pressurizing people are morally neutral. But, as MacIntyre says (p. 27),

in order to hold that such techniques are neutral, it is necessary also to hold that it is morally irrelevant whether a man comes to a given belief by reasoning or in some non-rational way. And in order to hold that this is morally irrelevant, one would have to hold also that a man's exercise of his rationality is irrelevant to his standing as a moral agent—irrelevant, that is, to deciding whether he is entitled to be called 'responsible' and his actions 'voluntary'.

Now, Gorgias revels in the superficial glibness of rhetoric. Why? Because he is wedded to the kinds of personal goals and lifestyle which go hand in hand with rhetoric. His teaching appeals to those who are anxious to make a name for themselves in the world, by wielding power over others. Gorgias acknowledges and delights in the fact that rhetoric is an instrument of power politics. At this point two further contrasts rear their heads and will play considerable parts in the dialogue: the contrast between the relative values of the outer world and one's inner life, and the related contrast between power over others and power over oneself, or self-control.

By the time Socrates' second interlocutor, Polus, takes over from Gorgias, then, the seeds have been sown which will develop in a typically Socratic fashion into an examination of how one ought to live. But first Socrates ties up a loose end by making explicit the superficiality of rhetoric: he denies it the name of *tekhnē* and prefers to call it a mere 'knack' (462c). Gorgias has claimed that its sphere of operation is right and wrong, but a rhetorician does not need knowledge of right and wrong. It is those who administer justice in a country's lawcourts and assemblies who have—or ideally have—knowledge of right and wrong (although Socrates would be the first to argue that terribly few of them do actually have such knowledge). Rhetoric is a counterfeit imitation of this branch of knowledge. It is limited to people's beliefs and to altering those beliefs, and according to Plato, that automatically condemns it to falling short of scientific status.

Polus is astonished at Socrates' low opinion of rhetoric and reintroduces the topic of power over others. The rest of the dialogue is now devoted to moral issues. The course of the arguments can be tracked through the italicized paragraphs which introduce each section of the dialogue, and there is some discussion of their validity in the notes. For our present purposes, the issues can be summarized quite succinctly. Polus approves of rhetoric because it gives one power over others, which is (he says) a route to happiness even if in the exercise of that power one behaves immorally or unjustly; Callicles approves of power over others because it allows one to indulge one's whims. Polus' function, then, is to argue that immoral or unjust behaviour is better for the agent than moral behaviour; Callicles' function is to argue that self-indulgent behaviour is better for the agent than behaviour which is self-controlled and takes other people into consideration. Socrates and Polus agree about what constitutes moral behaviour, but disagree about whether or not it makes one happy; Socrates and Callicles do not even share this point of agreement, however, since Callicles introduces a radical new conception of morality, which he claims is sanctioned by nature and which amounts to 'Might is right.'

Socrates' task is to maintain, against both these views, that virtue or moral goodness is more beneficial for the agent than the opposite. Virtue makes me happier than vice. A moment's thought will reveal how bold a thesis this is. We commonly think that moral behaviour is something we have to do as a kind of duty, even when it causes us some distress or at least inconvenience. But Plato is not half-hearted about the thesis. He wants us not just to behave morally, but to be moral people—to have an inner morality which acts as the basis for our outer behaviour. He believes that a moral person could be afflicted, like Job in the Bible, with every kind of torment and disaster, and still be happy, provided that he retains this state of morality. He believes, against Polus, that my doing wrong to others is actually incompatible with my being happy; and he believes, against Callicles, that my possession of unlimited license to satisfy my whims is also incompatible with happiness. Moreover, and perhaps most astonishingly, he claims that everybody already believes that morality and happiness are essentially interdependent: whatever people say, the view that morality causes happiness is in the last analysis—the kind of analysis Socratic argumentation provides—their deepest moral belief (475e).

*　　*　　*

In *Gorgias*, then, Plato faces us with two or three extreme points of view. A major part of the brilliance and fame of the dialogue is due to its vivid (and sometimes amusing) exposition of radical philosophical positions. At bottom, in fact, there are only two contrasting positions: firm adherence to outer, worldly goals and values, and firm adherence to inner goals and values (500c).

Some aspects of the contrast between inner and outer

life are more or less self-evident to a reader of the dialogue. Plato makes abundant play with it, both in developed argument and in unacknowledged allusions (such as the contrast between Socrates' likely aphasia in a worldly court—486a–b, 521e–522a—and Callicles' in the underworld court of 526e–527a). Gorgias, for instance, thinks that freedom consists in the ability to do what you feel like doing, even at the expense of others' freedom; in this he is followed closely by both Polus and Callicles. Socrates, however, thinks of our freedom primarily in terms of whether we have inner masters set over us. At the very least, we should have no addictions or strong needs; it would be better to have reduced our needs until we are content with whatever is to hand.

However, the central term of Greek moral vocabulary reflects the contrast in a way which would have been more obvious to a member of Plato's original audience than it might be to us. The term is *aretē*, which is usually translated 'virtue' or 'goodness'. It is the abstract noun associated with the adjective *agathos*, meaning 'good', and it therefore has as wide a range of applications as the adjective. We call a person morally good or good at weightlifting, we call a knife good if it is effective at cutting, we call a soup good if it is tasty, and so on. In origin, the word means 'the property of being male' (as, in fact, does the Latin *virtus*, from which we get the English 'virtue'). This reflects its original usage when applied to human beings. 'Virtue' was assessed by one's external behaviour, and particularly by one's achievements in society and battle. Later, as this heroic code became less relevant to Greek culture, the meaning of *aretē* changed somewhat, but still referred to external display—to holding high office in one's community, performing magnificent ritual offerings to the gods, and so on.

In the fifth century, and particularly in Athens, conditions encouraged the rise of a class of professional teachers who became known as the sophists. They supplemented the woefully inadequate schools by offering further education on a wide variety of topics. Their target audience consisted of wealthy, career-oriented young men who wanted to take advantage of the opportunities offered by the new democracy for advising the people and, in some cases, for personal advancement.

Now, the sophists too often claimed to be teaching *aretē* (519c). Since they were teaching people how to get on in the world in some way or another, they clearly accepted the normal Greek definition of *aretē* in terms of outer achievement. This is the context in which Socrates' interlocutors in *Gorgias* fit. Gorgias was explicitly teaching rhetoric to such career-oriented young men. Callicles' diatribe against the serious study and practice of philosophy (484c–486d) and his theme of playing Zethus to Socrates' Amphion (see the notes on 484e–486c and 506b) are Plato's brilliant ways of portraying a man protesting long and loud because he completely fails to understand the worth of the inner values championed by Socrates, for whom *aretē* was an inner state, manifesting in one's external behaviour. As Plato says in *Republic* (which develops and expands many of the themes of *Gorgias*), a person should first put his own inner house in order, and then he can take part in public life, if he wants (443c–444a; compare *Gorgias* 527d). There is nothing to be gained, and a great deal to be lost, by performing magnificent ritual offerings to the gods when your mind is actually corrupt and irreligious.

We can again see, from this point of view, why an attack on rhetoric was critical for Plato. It lay at the heart of the outer values accepted and perpetuated by Gorgias and others like him. It lay in direct contrast with the whole teaching of Socrates. Since its most important public manifestation was in the lawcourts and assemblies of Athens, where it told people what to do, it could plausibly claim to be involved with matters of right and wrong, justice and injustice. But to Plato's mind, philosophy offered the only authentic way of life, and it was philosophy which truly dealt with right and wrong. Rhetoric had to be swept out of the way, as a spurious rival. Tenkku says (pp. 61–2),

Plato assumes that ignorance of the true good is the main reason for the moral corruption of his time. The rhetoricians claim to know the greatest human good. Their answer to this fundamental question is nonetheless completely wrong, according to Plato. By means of persuasion rhetoric is, however, able to mislead people in this important matter. Thus, in attacking rhetoric, Plato fights against the very roots of evil.

*   *   *

Another recurrent term in the dialogue is 'happiness', which translates the Greek *eudaimonia* (literally, 'being in a good state'). Again, this is a very flexible term. All Greeks, however sophisticated or unsophisticated they were, would have accepted *eudaimonia* as a description of what they wanted to get out of life; they were all 'eudaemonists'. Where they differed, however, was over what constitutes happiness. Is it a life of sensual pleasure which brings happiness, or what?

In Greek, as in English, there is a natural connection between pleasure and happiness. We say, casually, 'Gardening makes me happy', meaning 'I enjoy gardening, I find it pleasant.' In *Gorgias*, however, Plato launches a strong attack against a type of hedonism, while simultaneously agreeing with the use of the term *eudaimonia* as a description of the aim of life. Moreover, in a dialogue which was certainly written not long before or after *Gorgias*— namely *Protagoras*—Socrates is made to espouse hedonism. We need to see what is going on.

It turns out that the topic of pleasure offers another route towards understanding Plato's dissatisfaction with rhetoric and the kinds of goals it entails. He makes it clear from the outset that he regards rhetoric and pleasure as essentially connected. He describes rhetoric as a species of flattery, and claims that flattery in all its guises aims for short-term pleasure rather than the good (464d). All you need in order to be a successful flatterer is enough experience of your human target to know what will please him or them (this is graphically portrayed at *Republic* 493a–c). So the problem with rhetoric is that it panders to its audience's short-term desires, and makes it difficult for them actually to think about what may or may not be better for them in the longer term.

Plato expresses the contrast at times very starkly. All branches of flattery aim only for pleasure, and all true *tekhnai* aim for the good of their subjects (464d–465a, 500a ff., 503a–b). He makes it sound as though pleasure and goodness are two incompatible things, so that one could only have one and not the other at the same time. However, I take it that the most accurate description of his position is that at 464d, where he says that branches of flattery are characterized by the fact that they aim for 'immediate pleasure'. This leaves open the possibility that long-term pleasure and goodness may still be related.

This is supported by a proper understanding of the anti-hedonist argument Socrates develops against Callicles (492d ff.). Again, Callicles is made out to be a champion of the immediate satisfaction of one's desires. His type of pleasure-seeker is entirely irrational: he doesn't allow the possibility of a person weighing up future pain against immediate pleasure and deciding to forgo that fifth cocktail. He doesn't allow the possibility of rational planning at all. If there is desire now for that fifth cocktail, then that desire had better be fulfilled if one is to be happy— that is Callicles' view, and that is the kind of hedonism which Plato and Socrates disavow. In fact, it is to Plato's credit that by means of the argument between Callicles and Socrates he allows us to distinguish between what may properly be called 'pleasure', and what should properly be called 'satisfaction of desire'.

This type of hedonism was, for Plato, self-contradictory, since it emphasizes the satisfaction of desire, which is a kind of pain or discomfort. The more intense the pleasure, the more intense the desire. Therefore, to seek to maximize this kind of pleasure is to seek to maximize one's physical discomfort. However, he has nothing against a less intense kind of pleasure, which is to be found in philosophical activities, as long as these activities involve no preceding perceived pain, so that the pleasant component easily outweighs the unpleasant component.

Throughout the dialogues (especially in *Republic* and *Philebus*) he expresses approval of these pleasures, and at *Gorgias* 499d ff. he expresses guarded approval of pleasures which promote genuine goods, such as health. The main differences between Plato and a Calliclean hedonist are that the latter seeks short-term gratification, whereas Plato looks for a life in which, in the long term, pleasure outweighs pain, and that a Calliclean hedonist makes desire-satisfaction his yardstick for assessing the goodness of an event, whereas for Plato pleasure was an accidental concomitant of events, which should in the first instance be assessed as good or bad by other criteria.

So it is possible to read *Gorgias* as maintaining the natural connection between happiness and pleasure, provided that certain qualifications are in place. The good life as recommended by Socrates in *Gorgias* need not be entirely devoid of pleasure, but it must be genuinely good for the agent. Indeed, it seems that Plato would argue that we can only really be said to *want* something if it is genuinely good for us (468c). Since by definition we all want happiness, then if this phrase 'want happiness' is not to be a solecism of some kind, happiness must be genuinely good for us; it follows, according to Plato, that we do not really want anything other than virtue. (Again we find the idea that, according to Plato, the position he attributes to Socrates in *Gorgias* is the one held in fact, whether or not they are initially aware of it, by everyone.) It also follows that the path to virtue must be rational— must be a *tekhnē*—since Plato effectively denies that we can be said to want happiness unless we can find some means towards the successful attainment of it (466b–468e), which involves the ability to distinguish between those pleasures which are good for us and those which are not (499d ff.). Since rhetoric is not a *tekhnē*, it cannot be a means to happiness.

*   *   *

We need to spell out in more detail what happiness consists in, according to Socrates. It consists in being moral,

xix

but the precise relationship between virtue and happiness in the Socratic dialogues is hard to ascertain. *Gorgias* is crucial, however, for the attempt to understand the relationship. Throughout the Socratic dialogues, Plato has Socrates assume some essential connection between virtue and happiness, but *Gorgias* is the only early or earlyish dialogue in which the connection is argued for at all.

Socrates agrees with his interlocutors that it is the possession of things that are good for a person which makes that person happy; where they differ is over what things are good for a person. Callicles thinks that unlimited sensual pleasure is good; we have already considered Socrates' disagreement with this view. Polus thinks it is good for one to have power over others, even to the extent of acting unjustly towards them; Socrates argues, by contrast, that immorality and injustice are bad for the agent, and even that they are worse for the agent than suffering the same injustice is to the sufferer.

Now if we consider even briefly the enormous evils that one can suffer unjustly, we can see how extraordinary this proposition is: one can be unjustly deprived of one's property, one can be unjustly expelled from one's city, one can have oneself and one's family unjustly enslaved, and one can be tortured unjustly, and unjustly be put to death . . . Socrates is arguing that in all these cases the man who does the injustice does thereby more harm to himself than the harm done to the sufferers of the injustice.

(Santas, p. 231)

This strand within *Gorgias* is of a piece with a Socratic principle, exemplified by a number of passages in other dialogues too, which has become known in the scholarly literature as the Principle of the Sovereignty of Virtue. This principle holds that virtue is by far the most valuable thing in life.

Whenever we must choose between exclusive and exhaustive alternatives which we have come to perceive as, respectively, just and unjust or, more generally, as virtuous and vicious, this very perception of them should decide our choice. Further deliberation would be useless, for none of the non-moral goods we might hope to gain, taken singly or in combination, could compensate us for the loss of a moral good. Virtue being the sovereign good in our domain of value, its claim upon us is always final.

(Vlastos, Socrates, pp. 210–11)

In modern colloquial English, talk of 'virtue' can sound rather stuffy and Victorian; it can smack of doing one's duty without flinching, without minding the inconvenience. We need to remind ourselves, then, that what determines the value of virtue is, according to Socrates, that it makes the agent happy. It is good *for me* to be moral; it is bad *for me* to be immoral. Like everyone else, I aim in all I do for my own happiness. Socrates is saying that virtue, properly understood, brings happiness in its train.

Virtue is intrinsically good, then; but is it the only good thing there is? There is some ambiguity in the evidence, but in the early dialogues Socrates usually counts other things as good as well as virtue. A rough list, in order of importance to Socrates, would include, after virtue, physical health, fitness and good looks, and adequate wealth and social standing. See, for instance, *Gorgias* 467e–468b, 477a ff., 499c–500a. However, as Vlastos has argued persuasively, the Principle of the Sovereignty of Virtue still remains in place. These things are good in the sense that, as long as they do not interfere with a moral life, they are on balance to be preferred over their opposites; but even so, their value compared with virtue is utterly insignificant. If I had virtue, I would still count as happy without them, although I would be slightly happier with them; and I would still count as miserable if I had these external goods in abundance, but was immoral.

Virtue is, on this view, the chief component of happiness. If asked what happiness consists in, Socrates would reply: above all, it consists in being moral and behaving morally. See his reply to Polus at 470e about the happiness of the Persian king. Other scholars (most notably Irwin), however, interpret the evidence differently. Rather than saying that virtue specifies, or all but specifies, the content of happiness, they say that the value of virtue is purely instrumental: it is a means to happiness.

A reader might think that this is all a scholarly storm in a teacup. Both interpretations, he or she might say, are simply claiming in different ways that virtue makes me happy. But there is rather more to it than that. I have already mentioned that in normal language, happiness and pleasure operate in much the same way. Now, consider the sentence, 'Gardening gives me pleasure.' The pleasure which gardening gives me is just the pleasure *of* gardening; it cannot be any other kind of pleasure, such as the pleasure of hang-gliding. Pleasure is, in technical terminology, an epiphenomenon; a given pleasure attends a given activity and no other activity.

Much the same is surely true of happiness (except that pleasure operates episode by episode, whereas happiness is more accurately assessed as an overall state). Happiness too is a state of being rather than an activity or set of activities. Its nature does not need extra specification: once you have specified the activity or activities which make you happy, you have gone as far as you can. Vlastos's interpretation satisfies this criterion: to say that virtue is the chief component of happiness is to say that happiness attends, above all, virtue. Irwin's instrumentalist interpretation, however, does not satisfy this criterion: it introduces such a gap between virtue and happiness that it is unclear what the content of happiness is. It is the equivalent of interpreting the sentence 'Gardening gives me pleasure' as if the pleasure was detachable from the gardening.

Although I have not seen precisely this criticism of the instrumentalist view before, it may not be out of place to assure the reader that a majority of scholars nowadays would agree that Irwin's instrumentalist view is incorrect. It relies heavily on a feature which he calls the Craft Analogy. According to the Craft Analogy, the knowledge which, Socrates repeatedly tells us, is virtue, is like craft knowledge: just as a craft has a definite product, so virtue has a product and that product is happiness. However, this over-emphasizes one aspect of Socrates' talk about 'craft' (*tekhnē*—see p. xi): not everything that is called a *tekhnē* has a product. Within *Gorgias*, for instance, purely theoretical disciplines such as mathematics are called *tekhnai* (450d). So it is certainly not clear that in likening virtue to *tekhnai* Plato means us to infer that virtue has a product, namely happiness. What Socrates seems to mean by the so-called 'paradox' that virtue is knowledge is that virtue involves knowledge of what is good and bad for oneself.

*   *   *

It needs to be made clear at this point that the term 'virtue' (or 'morality'), as used above, is actually a blanket term for two things—an inner psychological state and a kind of behaviour. In other words, although Plato often has Socrates talk as if the psychological state was all-important, he certainly did not mean us to think that we could be happy without also acting virtuously in relation to other people. A number of passages in *Gorgias* make it clear that such action is involved (503c–d, 507b–c, 513e, 515c–e, 517b–c; see also, for instance, *Republic* 335b–e). These passages also make it clear that when Socrates talks about virtuous actions, he means the kinds of action which are sanctioned by traditional morality and the laws of one's community—doing good to others, avoiding stealing, murdering, lying, and so on. To the extent, then, that Polus' and Callicles' ideas are subversive of traditional morality, Socrates may be seen as its champion.

The relative value of these two—the psychological state and moral behaviour—is unclear. While it is true that a psychological state of morality is a necessary prerequisite for genuinely moral action, Plato may also have thought that the inner state by itself has little or no value unless it is expressed in action. This is one possible interpretation of the assertion at *Crito* 47e (see also *Gorgias* 512a–b) that a chronically diseased body drastically reduces one's happiness. In short, then, it seems that Plato's Socrates is no quietist: happiness is impossible without virtuous activity. And since the chief component of happiness, as we have seen, is virtue, then this—the inner state—is impossible without external activity.

Now, virtuous behaviour is behaviour in relation to other people. It is unlikely that Socrates (or most other Greeks) would have gone as far as claiming that one should be motivated by altruism, because it was typically Greek to justify moral behaviour by arguing that it is good for the agent. Nevertheless, it is clear from *Gorgias* that virtuous behaviour in the external world is—naturally— expected to be good for others (see especially 503d–e, 515c–e, 517b–c). Yet we have seen that, for Socrates, to say that virtue is good is to say that it is beneficial for the agent. This is a constant throughout the dialogues: in our dialogue the idea is particularly prominent during the course of Socrates' discussion with Polus. How can we reconcile this egoism with moral behaviour towards others? The answer is plain from reflection on 506c ff. Socrates assumes there that inner morality and moral behaviour are inseparable: a moral person will indeed act well in relation to others. But since it is good for the agent to be moral, then if moral action is inseparable from being moral, it is good for me to behave morally towards others. This is a peculiar kind of egoism, to be sure: it has been dubbed 'moral egoism', and it is implicit throughout Plato's dialogues.

If we ask the important question as to why morality— the inner state and the outer actions—is good for me or makes me happy, Plato's answer is not particularly satisfactory, not so much because his argumentation is weak as because he rarely seems to address the question in the early dialogues (though the later *Republic* will be devoted to it). This is disappointing because

the relation of virtue to happiness is an important issue for any system of ethics in which happiness is both the final good and also the ultimate motive for all human action. For unless it can be shown that there is some significant connection between virtue and happiness (and vice and unhappiness), it will be difficult if not impossible both to justify the pursuit of virtue and to motivate men for it.

(Santas, pp. 218–19)

We could construct a prudential answer from considering the myth with which the dialogue concludes: it is good for me to avoid afterlife punishment. We could construct a different kind of prudential answer from occasional remarks such as the one at *Apology* 25c–e, where Socrates protests that it would be stupid of him to harm his fellow citizens, because that would make them worse people, and then he would have to live in the company of worse people, who would harm him in turn. This is probably related to the idea, casually introduced in our dialogue at 507e–508a, that an immoral person will be incapable of co-operating with the gods or his fellow human beings.

More commonly, however, in the early dialogues Plato simply takes it as self-evident that immorality is bad for one and morality is good. The word for 'virtue', remember, is *aretē*, which basically just means 'goodness'. Plato simply assumes that 'goodness' is a good or beneficial thing. One of the ways in which this assumption is evident in *Gorgias* is the recurrent analogy between a healthy body and a moral mind. This is never argued for in itself, but it is used repeatedly as a persuasive device or as an element in other arguments (see the note on 464c). One of these arguments comes close to being an argument about why morality makes me happy: at 464b–465d, and at 477a, it is argued that mental health is 'produced, preserved or recovered by the appropriate regimen of justice and legislation' (Zeyl, 'Socratic Virtue and Happiness', p. 233). Since mental health is good for me, and since the good and happiness are identical on Socrates' (as on any other) eudaemonistic theory, then justice makes me happy.

But the best argument we get for the idea that morality and happiness are essentially related comes from 506c ff. of our dialogue, where happiness is said to be the result of having an orderly mind. What orderliness means, in the first instance, is self-control, but both Socrates and Callicles see an essential connection between self-control and morality. A self-indulgent person thinks only of him- or herself, not others; a self-controlled person is therefore capable of other-regarding actions. To this extent, Socrates and Callicles agree. Where they disagree is over whether self-control or self-indulgence is good for me or makes me happy. Socrates argues that self-indulgence makes a person incapable of understanding what genuinely will make him or her happy. In Socrates' view, of course, it is morality as a whole which makes one happy; however, it is not a problem that this argument is couched chiefly in terms of self-control, which is only one aspect of virtue, because he believes that anyone who has one aspect of virtue has them all (507a–c; see also, and especially, *Protagoras*).

Still, the argument is rather abstract and elusive. The orderliness of the mind is directly likened to the orderliness of the component planks, ropes, and timbers of a ship (504a–b). What are the equivalent mental components, whose orderly arrangement constitutes self-control and makes one happy? The answer is probably the desires. If I restrain and reduce my desires, and perhaps adapt them to prevailing circumstances, then I will be capable of happiness. Moreover, if I marshal them—order them by giving some priority over others—by reference perhaps to which ones are realistic, and will give me on balance more pleasure than pain, and which do not interfere with my pursuit of virtue, then I will be capable of happiness. These are Socratic thoughts, to be sure, but they are not spelled out in the course of our dialogue, and our dialogue therefore remains deficient on the question of why morality makes me happy.

*   *   *

By the end of his arguments with Polus and Callicles, Socrates claims to have demonstrated that the moral life is the good life. Moreover, as has already been mentioned in passing (pp. xiv, xix), he claims to have shown that Polus and Callicles believed this all along and that all he has done is elicit the belief from them (see his remarks to Polus at 466e, 471e ff., 474b, and 475e, and to Callicles at 482b–c). This claim needs a little elucidation, especially since in combination with the fact that the belief happens to coincide with what Socrates himself believes, it begins to look not only arrogant, but dishonest, since Socrates often claims that the elenchus—as Socrates' argumentative technique has come to be known in the scholarly literature—is a search in which he is an ignorant participant. He claims that he himself lacks knowledge of the subject under investigation, and that he simply allows the logic of the argument to guide him and his interlocutors towards the inescapable conclusion.

Now, throughout the dialogue (as noted periodically in the notes—on 473b, 486e, and 509a), Socrates displays a remarkable confidence in his argumentative technique. The elenchus is the main feature of the Socrates we find in Plato's early dialogues (as opposed, say, to the Socrates of Xenophon's Socratic works). In order to understand this confidence, and to explain the appearance of arrogance, we need to examine the elenchus a bit.

The logical structure of the standard elenchus is straightforward. An interlocutor proposes a thesis (p); Socrates gains his assent to other theses (q, r, s . . .); Socrates demonstrates that $\{q, r, s\}$ themselves, or their consequences, contradict p; faced with a choice between p and *not-p*, the interlocutor gives up p.

As an example, consider the structure of the argument between Socrates and Polus at 466b–468e:

p Polus maintains that rhetoricians are powerful because they do what they want;

q Polus agrees that power is a good thing for its possessor;

r Polus agrees that we only ever want what is good for us.

Now, whatever the strengths and weaknesses of the argument Socrates develops against Polus (see the relevant notes on this section), it is clear that he uses Polus' assent to q

and *r* to argue that rhetoricians do not have power—i.e. *not-p*.

The question of Socrates' arrogance is, I think, a red herring. It depends on the status of *q* and *r* in the elenchus. If these propositions were idiosyncratic and peculiar to Socrates, then we would have grounds for accusing Socrates of arrogance (and probably of fast logical footwork too). In actual fact, though, they are probably meant to be so reasonable as to be more or less self-evident. They tend to be ideas which not only Socrates and his interlocutor agree to, but which any thinking Greek would agree to. They tend also to be generalizations like 'Courage is a fine thing.' Their eminent reasonableness is why Socrates' interlocutors, faced with a choice between abandoning *p* and denying *q* or *r*, invariably abandon *p*. They can hardly do otherwise. So I see no reason to conclude that Socrates is being arrogant just because the views he holds happen to remain unrefuted by the elenchus: they are supposed to be views we might all hold. However, what is important to Socrates is not that they are views *we* might hold, but that they are views which his interlocutor has no choice but to accept (see p. xi on the personal nature of the elenchus). Even in cases where *q* and *r* have the status of objective facts, so that the conclusion could plausibly be said to be true rather than simply consistent with an *ad hominem* argument, what is stressed by Socrates is the interlocutor's personal agreement with them, and the consistency of the set {*q*, *r*, *not-p*}.

There is another point of view, however, from which Socrates' confidence in the elenchus does start to seem extraordinary. It is clear from the structure of the elenchus, as displayed above, that it tests the consistency of the interlocutor's set of beliefs: he cannot simultaneously hold both *p* and {*q*, *r*, *s*} and remain consistent. Nevertheless, Socrates claims at several points in *Gorgias* that the elenchus enables him and his interlocutor to reach the *truth* (see 471e–472c, 479e, 486e, 487e, 508b, 508e–509a). Beliefs which remain unrefuted by the elenchus are held to be true beliefs.

Although this talk of truth is particularly prominent in *Gorgias*, it is neither unprecedented nor unwarranted by other Socratic dialogues. At *Charmides* 166d, for instance, Socrates claims that the facts can be revealed by elenchus, and at 175d he expresses sorrow that he and his interlocutors have been unable to discover the truth—which only makes sense on the assumption that he expected to be able to do so. Quite often in the early dialogues he prefaces arguments with the claim that they will establish the truth about whatever is being discussed. Therefore it makes sense to regard *Gorgias* in this context as of a piece with the earlier dialogues. Plato may by this stage have gained enough distance from the straightforwardly Socratic dialogues to be commenting on them; but he does not seem to be criticizing them (as Irwin believes, in 'Coercion and Objectivity').

But how can Socrates claim to be searching for truth when all he can reasonably expect to do is test for consistency? As Irwin trenchantly puts it (*Plato's Moral Theory*, p. 41): 'Whatever Socrates may think, the formal structure of the elenchus allows him to test consistency, not to discover truth. If I survive an elenchus with my original beliefs intact, I have some reason to believe they are consistent; but they may be consistently crazy.' Matters appear to be even worse when we consider *Gorgias* 480b. Here the idea that it is good for an immoral person to undergo punishment is accepted on the grounds that it is consistent with earlier conclusions; yet at 508a–509a this is one of the nest of ideas which is accepted as *true*. And there is evidence from elsewhere in the dialogues that Plato is aware that all these arguments can do is test for consistency; nevertheless, he still persists in having Socrates describe them as testing for truth. It is awkward, but it is undeniable, that Plato takes consistency to be a criterion of truth.

A number of solutions have been proposed to this difficulty. The one I propose is heavily indebted to some of Gregory Vlastos's ideas, though it is surprisingly not the solution he himself adopted to the problem. A somewhat fuller exposition of the solution can be found in the article of mine mentioned in the bibliography. The crux is that Socrates recognized two kinds or degrees of knowledge. On the one hand, there is the knowledge which experts have; on the other hand there is correctable or fallible knowledge, as exemplified in everyday speech, for instance, when a non-doctor says, 'I know it's unhealthy to smoke cigarettes.' An expert can reasonably be certain that he has a grasp on the truth of some matter. Correctable knowledge, however, is what Socrates believes the elenchus can produce. It is correctable in the sense that further bouts of the elenchus on the same issue may improve one's knowledge. To the extent that Socrates himself knows anything (as he occasionally claims to) or steers arguments in particular directions (which presupposes hunches, at the very least), he may claim to have correctable knowledge. At the same time, his disavowal of knowledge is sincere; he is a genuine participant in the search for more certain knowledge.

There is evidence from within *Gorgias* that Plato acknowledged these two degrees of truth. At 497c Socrates ironically applauds Callicles for his certainty about the issues under investigation. This certainty, he says, shows that Callicles has been initiated into the 'major mysteries' which are contrasted with the 'minor mysteries' of the elenchus.

Secondly, and perhaps even more remarkably, at 508b–509a, Socrates first claims that the conclusions have been proved true (a truth-claim like this is equivalent to a knowledge-claim), but then immediately goes on to make the profession of ignorance which is his trademark in *Gorgias* (see also 506a and 527d) as it is throughout the early dialogues. I take this to indicate that two different kinds of knowledge are being assumed. To use the language of a later philosophical dichotomy, Socrates remains ignorant about the nature of things, but knows how they appear to him.

In short, then, the truth which Socrates searches for by means of the elenchus is the kind of truth which accompanies consistency. A consistent set of beliefs, which incorporates notions which are reasonably held to be true, has a better chance of being true than an inconsistent set. Consistency is close to being the mark of a set of true beliefs; it is at least rationally compelling. Nevertheless, Plato is aware that this kind of truth falls short of absolute truth, which he attributes to genuine experts. However, there may even be a degree of irony in the claim to be searching for absolute truth, since it is evident from the early dialogues that Socrates believed that asking questions was at least as important as having answers; the possession of certainty on a topic closes doors and stops one searching further.

Finally, on this topic, we should note that to say that the elenchus can attain only a secondary degree of truth is not to say that it cannot achieve important results. The time is past when the elenchus could be seen only as an instrument Socrates used to puncture his interlocutors' conceit of knowledge. This is one of its functions, to be sure, but it is not the only one. Above all, what is important for Socrates is that the elenchus can affect the way a person lives, since no one wants to live by an inconsistent set of principles. Moreover, it can lead to a high degree of confidence in the propositions that survive the elenchus— the kind of confidence Socrates displays in *Gorgias*, as we have seen. If time and again, after repeated discussions (see 509a–b and perhaps 482a–b), the same ideas recur and survive the elenchus, then those ideas surely have some special status both in themselves and as guidelines to how to live one's life.

In the context of *Gorgias*, we may justly think that to award these ideas special status is absolutely essential. Time and again in the dialogue, Plato contrasts the methods of the elenchus with those of rhetoric (461d–462b, 471d–472c, 473e, 475e, 481d–482a). If all the elenchus can come up with, however, is plausible consistency, then philosophy (as exemplified by the elenchus) would hardly be preferable to rhetoric in this respect. This is no doubt why in our dialogue Plato places a great deal of emphasis on the idea that the elenchus can lead the way to truth. Even if it turns out on examination that a secondary kind of truth is meant, nevertheless Plato certainly leads us to understand that, unlike rhetoric, philosophy involves careful thought and rational procedure, and he expects that this is the only way the good will be attainable. As is often the case with *Gorgias*, this is another idea which will receive its full development in *Republic*.

In summary, the elenchus, as Brickhouse and Smith put it ('Socrates' Elenctic Mission', p. 159),

is a rich and complex enterprise in which one must purge others of their pretence of wisdom, undertake to determine what kinds of things people must believe about how to live if their lives are to be happy, test and refine definitions of the virtues, deliberate about right action, and when the nature of right and wrong action is clear enough, exhort others to pursue what is right and shun what is wrong. It is testimony to Socrates' genius as a moral philosopher that he turns the elenctic process into a vehicle by which his entire moral mission, in all its complexity, may be pursued, and which makes the dross of that process— those views that upon reflection even his interlocutors cannot accept—into the only evidence one needs for the pursuit of what all humans want, *eudaimonia*.

*   *   *

If we look back over *Gorgias*, a clear strategy emerges. The dialogue is about rhetoric because rhetoric is the paradigmatic activity which is concerned with *aretē* in the sense of success in the world. Thus it is a clear rival to philosophy which, in the hands of a Socrates or a Plato, is concerned with *aretē* as an inner state, first and foremost. One of Socrates' disciples, the philosopher Antisthenes, expressed the contrast succinctly: 'If you intend a boy to live with the gods, teach him philosophy; if you intend him to live with men, teach him rhetoric' (fr. 125 Mullach).

This contrast is the thread which unites the dialogue. Gorgias sows the seeds which develop into the crop of ideas proposed by Polus and Callicles. Socrates exposes both the original ideas and their ramifications as empty husks, containing no true happiness or fulfilment for a human being. To value rhetoric highly is to value the ability to manipulate others to do one's bidding. But this depends on a mistaken view about value. Socrates exposes the mistakes in order to establish the correct view, and so to suggest how we should live.

There is a curious twist here. Plato is obviously portraying Socrates at work on opponents whose views were subversive of traditional morality. Yet at the same time Socrates as usual becomes the champion of an inner-directed and individualistic morality which is itself subversive of convention to a high degree. He teaches us, as he taught his followers, to think for ourselves about moral issues, rather than to accept others' views, however well entrenched and sanctioned they may be; and he teaches that we should attend to ourselves first, because it is only if we are genuinely moral that we can help others to improve in the same direction through our involvement in politics or whatever (see 513e–514a, 521a, 521d—all this, of course, is again promissory of *Republic*). And this inward direction is potentially just as subversive of conventional morality as it is of Calliclean values, since both convention and Callicles put outer activity first.

In this way, two of the main strands of the early dialogues meet in *Gorgias*. It is common in the early dialogues for Socrates to probe, gently but ruthlessly, people's conventional ideas about morality, and he is also occasionally shown taking on a moral sceptic. The first group has accepted ideas thoughtlessly; the second has thought, but come to the wrong conclusions.

It is not the attempt to persuade others of their views that worries Plato where either of these two groups are concerned; after all, he is just as guilty of that (if it is a sin). What preoccupied him all his life, however, was that it is a feature of moral regulations and recommendations that they are trying to be objective; they are saying that their way is, or is ideally, the way people should live. It was very important for Plato to know whether and to what extent this claim, when put forward by either group, was correct—and this is plainly not a vacuous concern.

Against Gorgias, Polus, and Callicles, Plato pulls out all the stops. Gorgias' position is shown to be self-contradictory; Polus is muddle-headed; Callicles claims to be a free man, but is actually a slave to base desires. Socrates is far more certain of his position than in other early dialogues, and the dialogue ends with strong moral recommendations, not with uncertainty (which is how the Socratic dialogues commonly end).

There is, I think, a good dramatic–philosophical reason for this portrayal of certainty. Socrates' opponents in *Gorgias* are, as he ironically calls them at 527a, 'the three cleverest people in Greece today'. Moreover, they can offer clear tokens of what they call success; what can Socrates offer in return? 'To judge whether Archelaus is happy or unhappy, Polus is satisfied to look into Archelaus' court. Socrates needs to look into Archelaus' soul. He better have a clear enough view of happiness and unhappiness, and justice and injustice, to be able to judge what he finds there' (Santas, p. 253). That is why Socrates is portrayed by Plato as having clear views, for almost the first time in the series of dialogues. If *these* opponents confirm what Socrates has come to believe as a result of prior discussions (509a), then Socrates can confidently suppose that his moral code has a good claim to objectivity. This is why a recurrent theme of the dialogue concerns Socrates' interlocutors suffering, or potentially suffering, from embarrassment or attacks of propriety (see especially 461b–c, 482d–e, 494c–e, 508b–c). The feeling of embarrassment is created by the tension between what they profess to believe and live by, and the conflicting beliefs Socrates has uncovered within their minds—beliefs which he holds himself, and considers valid.

Gorgias is by far the longest of the early dialogues. This in itself suggests that Plato was aware of the importance of his task. In other Socratic dialogues, he has Socrates operate within a framework whose ultimate justification is that morality brings happiness and immorality unhappiness. *Gorgias* is a noble attempt to argue the point through. The overall result of the dialogue is that traditional morality best answers to human desires, provided that it stems from true inner virtue and is assisted by philosophy, so that it is approached and implemented rationally; only then can we be happy ourselves and make others happy as well. To prove this beyond the shadow of a doubt is an enormous task. Perhaps it is impossible— perhaps it is at bottom a matter of faith. But even if we find *Gorgias* in some respects less than convincing, we must surely applaud the attempt.

SELECT BIBLIOGRAPHY

Further books and articles are mentioned as appropriate in the notes at the end of the book. This bibliography contains only the works I consider the most important and helpful companions to reading *Gorgias*—works which are unlikely to be superseded for some time yet, or at least display a variety of interpretations.

A. *Translations*

The three best previous translations are:

HAMILTON, W., *Plato: Gorgias* (Harmondsworth: Penguin, 1960)
HELMBOLD, W. C., *Plato: Gorgias* (Indianapolis: Bobbs–Merrill, 1952)
ZEYL, D. J., *Plato: Gorgias* (Indianapolis: Hackett, 1987)

Two recent translations are rather plain and literal:

ALLEN, R. E., *The Dialogues of Plato* i. (New Haven: Yale University Press, 1984)
IRWIN, T., *Plato: Gorgias* (Oxford: Oxford University Press, 1979)

Nevertheless, Irwin's book is an essential companion to reading *Gorgias,* because the commentary is crammed with acute philosophical analysis of the text.

B. *Editions*

The only edition now worth consulting is:

DODDS, E. R., *Plato: Gorgias* (London: Oxford University Press, 1959)

C. *Plato in General*

Plato is set in his general ancient philosophical context, with admirable precision, by:

IRWIN, T., *Classical Thought* (Oxford: Oxford University Press, 1989)

The best introductions to and surveys of Plato's work as a whole are:

FIELD, G. C., *The Philosophy of Plato*, 2nd edn. (London: Oxford University Press, 1969)
GOSLING, J. C. B., *Plato* (London: Routledge & Kegan Paul, 1973)

GRUBE, G. M. A., *Plato's Thought* (London: Methuen, 1935)

HARE, R. M., *Plato* (Oxford: Oxford University Press, 1982)

And there is an outstanding collection of readable and informative essays:

KRAUT, R. (ed.), *The Cambridge Companion to Plato* (Cambridge: Cambridge University Press, 1992)

D. Socrates in General

Four scholarly books on Socrates which have a lot to contribute towards understanding *Gorgias* are:

REEVE, C. D. C., *Socrates in the Apology* (Indianapolis: Hackett, 1989)

SANTAS, G. X., *Socrates: Philosophy in Plato's Early Dialogues* (London: Routledge & Kegan Paul, 1979)

VLASTOS, G., *Socrates: Ironist and Moral Philosopher* (Cambridge: Cambridge University Press, 1991)

—— *Socratic Studies* (Cambridge: Cambridge University Press, 1994)

There are two good collections of essays:

BENSON, H. H. (ed.), *Essays on the Philosophy of Socrates* (Oxford: Oxford University Press, 1992)

VLASTOS, G. (ed.), *The Philosophy of Socrates: A Collection of Critical Essays* (Garden City: Anchor Books, 1971)

E. Rhetoric and the Sophists

The best book on the emerging art of rhetoric in ancient Greece is:

KENNEDY, G. A., *The Art of Persuasion in Greece* (Princeton: Princeton University Press, 1963)

Plato's views on rhetoric are discussed in a succession of essays in:

ERICKSON, K. V. (ed.), *Plato: True and Sophistic Rhetoric* (Amsterdam: Editions Rodopi, 1979)

Two books are worth mentioning on the sophistic movement in general, of which Gorgias was a leading light:

GUTHRIE, W. K. C., *A History of Greek Philosophy* iii. *The Fifth-century Enlightenment* (Cambridge: Cambridge University Press, 1969). This was issued in 1971 by the same publisher in two separate parts: *The Sophists* and *Socrates*.

KERFERD, G. B., *The Sophistic Movement* (Cambridge: Cambridge University Press, 1981)

The best piece of work, to my mind, on Gorgias' precise relation to the sophistic movement is:

HARRISON, E. L., 'Was Gorgias a Sophist?', *Phoenix* 18 (1964), 183–92

F. *The Dialogue: Background Reading*

The main phases of the dialogue as a whole are surveyed and discussed, from very different points of view, in:

GUTHRIE, W. K. C., *A History of Greek Philosophy* iv. *Plato, the Man and His Dialogues: Earlier Period* (Cambridge: Cambridge University Press, 1975), 284–312

KAHN, C. H., 'Drama and Dialectic in Plato's *Gorgias*', *Oxford Studies in Ancient Philosophy* 1 (1983), 75–121

MCKIM, R., 'Shame and Truth in Plato's *Gorgias*', in C. L. Griswold (ed.), *Platonic Writings, Platonic Readings* (New York: Routledge, Chapman & Hall, 1988), 34–48, 272–4

Like all Plato's early dialogues, *Gorgias* is concerned above all with ethical questions. It is invaluable to start by knowing something of the background:

DOVER, K. J., *Greek Popular Morality in the Time of Plato and Aristotle* (Oxford: Basil Blackwell, 1974)

The best introduction to the history of ethical thought (with a short chapter devoted to *Gorgias*) is:

MACINTYRE, A., *A Short History of Ethics* (London: Routledge & Kegan Paul, 1967)

Useful introductions to Greek philosophical ethics are:

PRIOR, W. J., *Virtue and Knowledge: An Introduction to Ancient Greek Ethics* (London: Routledge, 1991)

ROWE, C. J., *An Introduction to Greek Ethics* (London: Hutchinson, 1976)

A tough, controversial, and outstanding book on Plato's moral theories (and more besides) is:

IRWIN, T., *Plato's Moral Theory: The Early and Middle Dialogues* (Oxford: Oxford University Press, 1977)

G. *The Dialogue and Socratic Ethics*

See also the items mentioned in section D. Some papers focus on some phases of the dialogue more than others, but still extract broad implications for the dialogue, or even for Socrates' moral philosophy as a whole:

BERMAN, S., 'Socrates and Callicles on Pleasure', *Phronesis* 36 (1991), 117–40

PENNER, T., 'Socrates on the Impossibility of Belief-relative Sciences', *Proceedings of the Boston Area Colloquium on Ancient Philosophy* 3 (1987), 263–325

—— 'Desire and Power in Socrates: The Argument of *Gorgias* 466a–468e That Orators and Tyrants Have No Power in the City', *Apeiron* 24 (1991), 147–202

WHITE, N. P., 'Rational Prudence in Plato's *Gorgias*', in D. J. O'Meara (ed.), *Platonic Investigations* (Washington: Catholic University of America Press, 1985), 139–62

Plato's arguments about pleasure and hedonism in *Gorgias* are discussed in:

GOSLING, J. C. B., and TAYLOR, C. C. W., *The Greeks on Pleasure* (Oxford: Oxford University Press, 1982)

RUDEBUSCH, G., 'Plato, Hedonism and Ethical Protagoreanism', in J. P. Anton and A. Preus (eds.), *Essays in Ancient Greek Philosophy* iii, *Plato* (Albany: State University of New York Press, 1989), 27–40

TENKKU, J., *The Evaluation of Pleasure in Plato's Ethics* (Helsinki: Societas Philosophica, 1956 = *Acta Philosophica Fennica* 11)

The crucial question of the relation between virtue and happiness in the early Platonic dialogues is discussed by:

BRICKHOUSE, T. C., and SMITH, N. D., 'Socrates on Goods, Virtue and Happiness', *Oxford Studies in Ancient Philosophy* 5 (1987), 1–27

IRWIN, T., 'Socratic Puzzles', *Oxford Studies in Ancient Philosophy* 10 (1992), 241–66

KLOSKO, G., 'Socrates on Goods and Happiness', *History of Philosophy Quarterly* 4 (1987), 251–64

WHITE, F. C., 'The Good in Plato's *Gorgias*', *Phronesis* 35 (1990), 117–27

ZEYL, D. J., 'Socratic Virtue and Happiness', *Archiv für Geschichte der Philosophie* 64 (1982), 225–38

H. *Method and Moral Certainty*

Gorgias offers a great many insights into Socrates' method of argument (the elenchus) and his use of it to try to attain truth and moral certainty. Since the method is typical of Socrates, items mentioned in section D will again be relevant. The starting-point for considering the elenchus is still:

ROBINSON, R., *Plato's Earlier Dialectic*, 2nd edn. (London: Oxford University Press, 1953)

A more recent watershed was a typically brilliant and controversial article by Gregory Vlastos:

VLASTOS, G., 'The Socratic Elenchus', *Oxford Studies in Ancient Philosophy* 1 (1983), 27–58
—— 'Afterthoughts on the Socratic Elenchus', *Oxford Studies in Ancient Philosophy* 1 (1983), 71–4

Since then, there have been a number of studies of the issues, of which I would single out the following:

BRICKHOUSE, T. C., and SMITH, N. D., 'Vlastos on the Elenchus', *Oxford Studies in Ancient Philosophy* 2 (1984), 185–95
—— —— 'Socrates' Elenctic Mission', *Oxford Studies in Ancient Philosophy* 9 (1991), 131–59
IRWIN, T., 'Coercion and Objectivity in Plato's Dialectic', *Revue internationale de philosophie* 156–7 (1986), 49–74
KRAUT, R., 'Comments on Gregory Vlastos, "The Socratic Elenchus"', *Oxford Studies in Ancient Philosophy* 1 (1983), 59–70
POLANSKY, R., 'Professor Vlastos' Analysis of Socratic Elenchus', *Oxford Studies in Ancient Philosophy* 3 (1985), 247–59
SCALTSAS, T., 'Socratic Moral Realism: An Alternative Justification', *Oxford Studies in Ancient Philosophy* 7 (1989), 129–50
WATERFIELD, R. A. H., 'Truth and the Elenchus in Plato', in P. Huby and G. Neal (eds.), *The Criterion of Truth* (Liverpool: Liverpool University Press, 1989), 39–56

GORGIAS

I have translated the Greek text of E. R. Dodds, *Plato: Gorgias* (London: Oxford University Press, 1959), except at 493b2 and 510c3.

The numbers and letters that appear in the margins are the standard means of precise reference to Plato. They refer to the pages and sections of pages of the edition of Plato's works by Stephanus (Henri Estienne), published in Geneva, 1578.

Socrates and his friend Chaerephon arrive outside an unnamed person's house, just too late to hear the sophist and orator Gorgias, who is visiting Athens from his home town of Leontini in Sicily. They chat to their acquaintance Callicles at the front door, and then move inside. Gorgias is drawn into conversation with Socrates. The characterizations of Gorgias and his disciple Polus are deft and amusing.

CALLICLES: This is how you're supposed to turn up when 447a there's a war on or a battle to be fought, Socrates.

SOCRATES: You mean we've done the proverbial thing and arrived when the feast is over? Are we too late?

CALLICLES: Yes, and a very nice feast it was too. Gorgias has just finished presenting a number of fine pieces.*

SOCRATES: Here's the culprit, Callicles: it's all Chaerephon's fault. He made us waste time in the agora.

CHAEREPHON: Never mind, Socrates. I'll make things b better as well, because Gorgias is a friend of mine. I'm sure he'll present some of his work for us—now or another time, whichever you'd prefer.

CALLICLES: What's that, Chaerephon? Does Socrates really want to listen to Gorgias?

CHAEREPHON: Yes, that's exactly why we're here.

CALLICLES: Well, Gorgias is staying with me and you're welcome to visit any time you like. He'll put on a presentation for you.

SOCRATES: Thanks, Callicles. But do you think he'd be prepared to carry on a conversation with us?* He c professes and teaches a particular branch of expertise, and I want to ask him what it is and what it can do. He can leave the rest of his presentation for another occasion, as you suggested.

CALLICLES: There's nothing like asking the man himself, Socrates. Actually, you've mentioned something that formed part of his presentation. Just a moment ago he was inviting questions on anything anyone here in the house cared to ask him, and he claimed that he'd answer them all.

SOCRATES: That's wonderful . . . You ask him, Chaerephon.

CHAEREPHON: What?

d SOCRATES: Who he is.

CHAEREPHON: What do you mean?

SOCRATES: Well, if making shoes was his job, he'd reply to your question by saying, 'I'm a shoe-maker.' Do you see what I mean?

CHAEREPHON: Yes. All right, I'll ask him. Can you tell me, please, Gorgias, whether Callicles here is telling the truth when he says that you claim to be able to answer any question that's put to you?

448a GORGIAS: He is, Chaerephon. That's exactly what I was doing a short while ago, in fact, and I'll add that for many years now I've never been faced with a question I hadn't met before.

CHAEREPHON: Then you'll find it easy to answer my question, Gorgias, I'm sure.

GORGIAS: Here's your opportunity to find out, Chaerephon.

POLUS: I honestly think you should put your questions to me, Chaerephon, if you don't mind. I get the impression that Gorgias is tired. He's just finished a long teaching session.

CHAEREPHON: Do you really think you'll give me better answers than Gorgias, Polus?

b POLUS: What's the difference, as long as they're good enough for you?

CHAEREPHON: None at all. Here's my question, then, since that's what you want.

POLUS: Go on.

CHAEREPHON: All right. If Gorgias happened to be in the same line of business as his brother Herodicus,

4

we'd have to call him the same as we call his brother, wouldn't we?

POLUS: Yes.

CHAEREPHON: In other words, we'd have to call him a doctor.

POLUS: Yes.

CHAEREPHON: And if his professional experience was in the same field as Aristophon the son of Aglaophon, or his brother, what would it be right to call him?

POLUS: A painter, obviously.   c

CHAEREPHON: What is his area of expertise, in actual fact? What would it be right to call him?

POLUS: Chaerephon, experience and experimentation have led people to develop professional expertise in a number of areas. Experience brings expertise to the process of human existence, while inexperience leaves it haphazard. Now, there are various areas of expertise, variously practised by various people, but the best are in the hands of the best practitioners. Gorgias here is one of them, and the area of expertise in which he is engaged is the finest there is.*

SOCRATES: It certainly looks as though Polus is well d qualified to speak, Gorgias, but he's not doing what he promised Chaerephon he'd do.

GORGIAS: Why's that, Socrates?

SOCRATES: He doesn't really seem to me to be answering the question.

GORGIAS: Why don't you question him, then, if you want?

SOCRATES: I don't want to if there's a chance that *you* might be willing to answer my questions. I'd much rather ask you. I mean, I can tell from Polus' speech that he's more interested in rhetoric, as it's called, than in carrying on a conversation.

POLUS: What gives you that impression, Socrates?   e

SOCRATES: Because when Chaerephon asks you what Gorgias' area of expertise is, Polus, you come out with a eulogy of it—as if someone had been running it down—instead of telling us what it is.

POLUS: But didn't I say that it's the finest area of expertise there is?

SOCRATES: You certainly did, but no one asked you what *qualities* Gorgias' area of expertise has. The question was what it is, and what Gorgias should be called. You gave excellent, concise answers to the questions Chaerephon had previously put to you, so

449a couldn't you do the same now, and tell us what Gorgias' area of expertise is and what we should call him? Or rather, Gorgias, won't you tell us yourself what your area of expertise is, and so what to call you?

GORGIAS: It's rhetoric, Socrates.

SOCRATES: We'd better call you a rhetorician, then?

GORGIAS: A good one, Socrates, if you want to call me what (as Homer puts it) 'I avow I am.'*

SOCRATES: I'll gladly do so.

GORGIAS: Then that's what you can call me.

b SOCRATES: What about training other people in rhetoric too? Should we attribute this ability to you?

GORGIAS: Yes, that's what I offer to do, here in Athens and elsewhere as well.

SOCRATES: Now, would you mind if our discussion continued the way it's begun, Gorgias, with you asking a question here and answering one there? Would it be all right with you if we postponed the kind of lengthy speech-making which Polus introduced? Please keep your promise and give short answers to questions.

GORGIAS: Some questions need long speeches to answer them, Socrates, but all the same I'll try to keep my

c answers as short as possible. In fact, that's another of my claims—that no one can find a more concise way to express an idea than me.

SOCRATES: That's what we need, Gorgias. A display of precision is exactly what I'd like from you, and longwindedness can wait.

GORGIAS: All right. I'll leave you in no doubt that what you're hearing is as precise as it gets.

6

Socrates asks what Gorgias' area of expertise, rhetoric, is concerned with. Gorgias says 'speech', but Socrates argues, first, that all areas of expertise are concerned to some extent with speaking, and, second, that a number of other areas of expertise are as essentially concerned with speech as rhetoric is. Gorgias' first attempt at defining rhetoric fails because it is too wide. The Greek for 'spoken word' (logos) is also the Greek for 'written word', but a modern reader should bear in mind that for the Greeks speech was far more primary than it is for us today. Logos also means 'account', 'argument', 'definition', and 'rational explanation' (as distinct from a story); all these translations will occur in the course of the dialogue.

SOCRATES: Here we go, then. Now, you describe yourself as an expert in rhetoric and you also claim to
pass it on to other people too. But what aspect of life d
is rhetoric concerned with? The province of weaving,
for instance, is the manufacture of clothes, wouldn't
you say?

GORGIAS: Yes.

SOCRATES: And music is concerned with the composition of tunes?

GORGIAS: Yes.

SOCRATES: I'm really impressed with your answers,
Gorgias. I can't imagine how they could be shorter.

GORGIAS: Yes, I think I'm doing pretty well, Socrates.

SOCRATES: You're right. Now then, I'd like to hear what
you have to say in the same vein about rhetoric as
well. What aspect of life does *it* know about?

GORGIAS: Speaking.   e

SOCRATES: In what sense, Gorgias? Do you mean ex-
plaining to people when they're ill what regimen to
follow to get better?

GORGIAS: No.

SOCRATES: In that case, rhetoric isn't concerned with *all*
speech.

GORGIAS: No, of course not.

SOCRATES: But it does make people competent at speaking.

GORGIAS: Yes.

SOCRATES: And also at understanding what they're speaking about?

GORGIAS: Naturally.

450a SOCRATES: Now, isn't it expertise in medicine, which we referred to a moment ago, which makes one competent at understanding and speaking about people who are ill?

GORGIAS: Of course.

SOCRATES: So it seems to follow that medicine is concerned with speaking too.*

GORGIAS: Yes.

SOCRATES: With speaking about illness, anyway. Yes?

GORGIAS: Definitely.

SOCRATES: Would you say, then, that physical education is also concerned with speaking—with speaking about physical fitness and unfitness?

GORGIAS: Yes.

SOCRATES: And the same goes for every other area of expertise as well, Gorgias. Every single one of them
b is concerned with speech, when the matter being talked about happens to be the one which is the province of its particular expertise.

GORGIAS: I suppose so.

SOCRATES: Given that you're defining rhetoric as the area of expertise which is concerned with speech, then, why don't you describe *any* form of expertise as rhetoric, since expertise and speaking *always* go together?

GORGIAS: Because the knowledge which other areas of expertise possess is more or less entirely confined to manual work and that kind of activity, whereas there is no element of manual work in rhetoric. It relies entirely on the spoken word in performing its task
c and achieving its results. That's why I maintain that the province of rhetoric is speech, and—as I say—I think I'm right.

SOCRATES: I'm not sure I understand what you're trying

8

to say about rhetoric, but perhaps it'll become clear later. Here's a question for you, though. We've got these areas of expertise, right?

GORGIAS: Yes.

SOCRATES: Well, some of them are largely taken up with practical activity and have little need of speaking. In fact, some of them don't need the spoken word at all: even complete silence wouldn't stop them accomplishing whatever it is their expertise is for. I'm thinking here of painting, sculpture, and so on and so forth. I suppose these are the kinds of areas of expertise you were talking about when you said that there are some which rhetoric bears no relation to. d Or am I wrong?

GORGIAS: No, you're quite right, Socrates.

SOCRATES: Then there are other areas of expertise which rely entirely on speech for their accomplishments. In these cases it's hardly an exaggeration to say that practical action isn't important to them at all, or isn't particularly important. I'm thinking of mathematics, for instance, and arithmetic and geometry—not forgetting backgammon*—and there are plenty of others as well. Some of them give more or less equal weight to words and action, but most of them favour words and in general rely exclusively on them in performing their tasks and achieving their results. e *These* are the kinds of areas of expertise among which you're counting rhetoric, I take it.

GORGIAS: You're right.

SOCRATES: But I'm sure you wouldn't want actually to identify rhetoric with any of them. I know that's what it sounded as though you were saying, when you defined rhetoric as the area of expertise which relies on speech to achieve its results, and if someone wanted to pick a quarrel he might take you up on this point and say, 'So you're identifying rhetoric with mathematics, are you, Gorgias?' But I'm sure you're not actually identifying rhetoric with mathematics or geometry.

9

451a GORGIAS: You're right, Socrates. You've correctly interpreted my meaning.

*Socrates suggests that Gorgias can retain his descrip-
tion of rhetoric, but should narrow it down by pin-
pointing its particular domain or subject-matter. Gorgias
replies grandiosely that rhetoric is concerned with the
most important aspects of human life, by which he
turns out to mean politics. Rhetoric is the art of persuading others to do what you want them to do, especially in the political arena. Socrates continues to prod
Gorgias until he narrows the sphere of rhetoric down
further, to morality, and then further still to: 'Rhetoric
is an agent of the kind of persuasion which is designed
to produce conviction, but not to educate people, about
matters of right and wrong.'*

SOCRATES: All right, then, please will you finish answering my question yourself, in the terms in which I
asked it. Given that rhetoric is one of those areas of
expertise which rely heavily on the spoken word, but
that there are in fact others which fit this description
too, please try to tell us what the particular province
is in which rhetoric achieves its results by means of
speech. Here's an example. Imagine someone taking
me up on one of the areas of expertise I mentioned
a moment ago and asking, 'What is mathematics,
b   Socrates?'
'It's one of the areas of expertise which rely on
words to achieve their results,' I'd tell him, copying
the reply you gave us a short while ago.
'But what is it concerned with?' he'd go on to ask.
'Odd and even numbers of any quantity,' I'd
answer.
'And what do you call arithmetic?' he'd ask next.
'That's another area of expertise which relies on
words to achieve its results,' I'd say.
'And what does it deal with?' he'd continue.
My reply would sound like a political statute:
c   'Whereas in some respects arithmetic resembles

10

mathematics—in that they are both concerned with odd and even numbers—nevertheless there is this difference between them, that arithmetic investigates the quantitative relationships that odd and even numbers form between themselves and one another.'

And suppose it was astronomy which was the subject of his next question, and I described it as another area of expertise which relies on words for all its results. And suppose he asked, 'But what are astronomers' words *about*, Socrates?', I'd reply, 'They're concerned with the movements of the sun, moon, and other heavenly bodies, and their relative speeds.'

GORGIAS: And you'd be right, Socrates.

SOCRATES: All right, Gorgias, it's your turn. Rhetoric is d one of those areas of expertise which rely on the spoken word for all their accomplishments and achievements. Yes?

GORGIAS: Yes.

SOCRATES: Please tell us, then, what its province is. What aspect of life is the rhetorical use of the spoken word concerned with?

GORGIAS: The most important and valuable aspect of human life, Socrates.

SOCRATES: Now, here's another idea of yours, Gorgias, which is open to question and in need of a great deal of clarification. For instance, I'm sure you've heard e the song people sing at parties which offers a list of human advantages: 'The very best thing is health, second good looks, and third'—according to whoever made up the song—'honest wealth.'*

GORGIAS: Yes, I have. But why are you bringing it up?

SOCRATES: Well, suppose a doctor, a trainer, and a busi- 452a nessman—who are the people responsible for the qualities the song-writer commended—were standing right there next to you. And suppose the doctor went first and said, 'Socrates, Gorgias isn't telling you the truth. The greatest of human blessings isn't covered by his area of expertise, but by mine.'

11

'You say it's your province,' I'd reply, 'but what are you?'

'I'm a doctor,' he'd presumably answer.

'What do you mean? Is your area of expertise responsible for the greatest of human blessings?'

'Of course, Socrates,' he'd probably reply, 'because its product is health. And what could be better for people than health?'

b

And imagine the trainer going next and saying, 'Listen, Socrates, if Gorgias can show you that the product of his area of expertise is more beneficial for people than I can show mine to be, I'd share the doctor's surprise.'

I'd ask him the same question as before: 'Who are you, sir? What's your job?'

'I'm a trainer,' he'd reply, 'and my job is making people's bodies attractive and fit.'

And then it would be the businessman's turn to speak, and I see his attitude as one of total disdain.

c

'I want you to consider, Socrates,' he'd say, 'whether you really think that anything which Gorgias or anyone else can procure is more beneficial than wealth.'

'What?' we'd say. 'Is wealth yours to produce?'

'Yes.'

'What are you, then?'

'A businessman.'

'And in your opinion people can have no greater advantage than wealth?' we'll ask.

'Of course they can't,' he'll reply.

'But Gorgias here doesn't agree,' we'd point out. 'He claims that his area of expertise is responsible for something which is more beneficial than anything yours can produce.'

And the businessman's next question will obviously be: 'What is this wonderful thing? Gorgias had

d

better tell us.'

So, Gorgias, please add their imagined request to mine, and tell us what this thing is which is the

12

greatest blessing people can have, according to you, and which you can procure for them.

GORGIAS: When I say there's nothing better, Socrates, that is no more than the truth. It is responsible for personal freedom and enables an individual to gain political power in his community.

SOCRATES: Yes, but what *is* it?

GORGIAS: I'm talking about the ability to use the spoken e word to persuade—to persuade the jurors in the courts, the members of the Council, the citizens attending the Assembly*—in short, to win over any and every form of public meeting of the citizen body. Armed with this ability, in fact, the doctor would be your slave, the trainer would be yours to command, and that businessman would turn out to be making money not for himself, but for someone else—for *you* with your ability to speak and to persuade the masses.

SOCRATES: Gorgias, I think you've finally come very close to revealing what you think rhetoric does. If I've 453a understood you correctly, you're saying that rhetoric is the agent of persuasion—that persuasion is the sum total and the fundamental goal of all its activity. Is that right? Or do you want to claim that rhetoric has further abilities, apart from winning over the minds of an audience?

GORGIAS: No, Socrates, I don't. I think you've described it well enough. That is fundamentally what rhetoric does.

SOCRATES: Well, I've got something to tell you, Gorgias. You should be aware that I'm a prime example—or so I'm persuaded—of the type of person who en- b gages in conversation purely because he wants to understand the topic under discussion. I'm like that myself, I believe, and I hope you are too.

GORGIAS: Why, Socrates?

SOCRATES: I'll tell you straight away. The point is, you see, that I don't fully understand what this rhetoric-based persuasion you're talking about is, and what it

13

is persuasion *about*. This is not to say that I don't at least have a vague idea of what you mean it to be, and what its sphere of operation is, but all the same I'm going to ask you to explain what this rhetoric-based persuasion is and what its province is. You may wonder why I'm asking you for an explanation, and not stating my own view of the matter, however vague that may be. It doesn't actually have anything to do with you; I just want the course of the discussion to show us as clearly as possible what it is we're talking about. I think you'll agree that it's fair for me to question you if you look at it this way. Suppose my question had actually been what sort of painter Zeuxis is, and you'd replied that he paints figures, wouldn't it be fair for me to have asked you what kinds of figures he paints, and where his work can be seen?

GORGIAS: Yes.

d SOCRATES: And it would be fair because there are other painters who paint a wide variety of different kinds of figures?

GORGIAS: Yes.

SOCRATES: Whereas if Zeuxis were the only painter in the world, your answer would have been fine. Yes?

GORGIAS: Of course.

SOCRATES: All right. Now, what about rhetoric? Is rhetoric the only area of expertise whose product is persuasion, do you think, or are there others too? Here's what I'm getting at. Is it or isn't it the case that any teacher of any subject persuades his students of what he's trying to get them to understand?

GORGIAS: Of course he does, Socrates. Persuasion is essential to teaching.

e SOCRATES: Let's have another look, in this context, at the same areas of expertise we were talking about a short while ago. Doesn't mathematics teach us the properties of number? Isn't that what a mathematician does?

GORGIAS: Yes.

14

SOCRATES: And doesn't he persuade us about them as well?

GORGIAS: Yes.

SOCRATES: It follows that mathematics is another agent of persuasion.

GORGIAS: I suppose so.

SOCRATES: Now, if we were asked what kind of persuasion it is an agent of, and what it is persuasive about, we'd presumably answer that it is an agent of educational persuasion, and that its province is odd and even numbers and their quantities. And we could do 454a the same for all the other areas of expertise we mentioned a short while ago—we could show not just that they are agents of persuasion, but also what particular kind of persuasion they are agents of, and what their spheres of operation are. Do you agree?

GORGIAS: Yes.

SOCRATES: So rhetoric isn't the only agent of persuasion.

GORGIAS: You're right.

SOCRATES: Well, given that other areas of expertise produce the same result and rhetoric isn't an isolated case, wouldn't it be fair for us next to ask the same question we asked about Zeuxis and his painting? Faced with the claim that rhetoric is an agent of persuasion, we should ask, 'Yes, but what kind of persuasion does rhetoric produce, and what is its sphere of operation?' Don't you think that's a fair question? b

GORGIAS: Yes, I do.

SOCRATES: In that case, Gorgias, please will you answer it?

GORGIAS: Well, Socrates, I think—to repeat what I was saying not long ago—that its effect is to persuade people in the kinds of mass meetings which happen in lawcourts and so on; and I think its province is right and wrong.

SOCRATES: Actually, you've exactly confirmed my suspicions, Gorgias, about the sort of persuasion you meant

15

and its province as well. Now, I hope you won't be
surprised if a little later I ask you the same kind of
question again—the kind of question which asks for
further clarification, when something seems to be clear

c already. As I say, there's nothing personal in these
questions; they're only meant to let the discussion
proceed in due order, and to stop us getting into the
habit of pre-empting the other person's meaning as a
result of having half-formed ideas about it. I just
want you to be able to develop your own views—in
keeping with whatever you had in mind at the outset—in your own preferred way.

GORGIAS: I certainly can't see anything wrong with that,
Socrates.

SOCRATES: All right, then. Here's something else for us
to think about. You do recognize that there are situations when we say 'I've been taught', don't you?

GORGIAS: Yes.

SOCRATES: And also when we say 'I'm convinced'?

GORGIAS: Yes.

d SOCRATES: Now, do you think that the state of having
been taught something is the same as the state of
having been convinced? Is learning the same as conviction, or different?

GORGIAS: In my opinion, Socrates, they're different.

SOCRATES: Yes, you're right, and here's the proof of it.
If you were asked, 'Gorgias, can conviction be either
true or false?', you'd answer yes, I'm sure.

GORGIAS: Yes.

SOCRATES: But can knowledge be either true or false?

GORGIAS: Certainly not.

SOCRATES: Obviously, then, conviction and knowledge
aren't the same.

GORGIAS: Right.

e SOCRATES: All the same, it isn't only people who've
learned something who have been persuaded of it;
people who've been convinced of something have as
well.

GORGIAS: True.

16

SOCRATES: So we'd better think in terms of two kinds of persuasion, one of which confers conviction without understanding, while the other confers knowledge.

GORGIAS: All right.

SOCRATES: Which of these two kinds of persuasion, then, in the province of right and wrong, is the effect rhetoric has on people when they're assembled in lawcourts and so on? Is it the kind which leads to conviction without understanding, or the kind which leads to understanding?

GORGIAS: The answer's obvious, Socrates: it's the kind that leads to conviction.

SOCRATES: It turns out, then, that rhetoric is an agent of the kind of persuasion which is designed to produce 455a conviction, but not to educate people, about matters of right and wrong.

GORGIAS: Yes.

SOCRATES: A rhetorician, then, isn't concerned to educate the people assembled in lawcourts and so on about right and wrong; all he wants to do is persuade them. I mean, I shouldn't think it's possible for him to get so many people to understand such important matters in such a short time.

GORGIAS: No, that's right.

Against the background of this definition of rhetoric, Socrates argues that it is of limited value. Most aspects of life are covered by specialists, to whom we turn when we need advice. Gorgias acknowledges the role of specialists, but replies that rhetoric influences events and then hands them over to the various specialists. A rhetorician could even persuade people that he was a specialist of some kind, when he wasn't. However, Gorgias quickly explains that he's not recommending this kind of abuse of the immense power of rhetoric and concludes that when that happens one should blame the practitioner, not people like himself, who merely teach rhetoric.

17

SOCRATES: Come on, then, let's see what it is we're
b actually saying about rhetoric. You see, I have to tell
you that *I* can't yet make up my mind what to think
about it. When there's a public meeting in Athens to
elect a doctor or a shipwright or any other professional, the purpose of the meeting is obviously to
choose the person with the greatest expertise for each
post, so it's not going to be a rhetorician who advises
them under these circumstances, is it? They're not
going to use rhetoricians to advise them when there
are fortifications to be built or harbours or dockyards to be constructed: they'll use master builders.
Again, they're not going to use rhetoricians to advise
them on who to elect to military command or on
troop movements in combat or on capturing enemy
c territory: it'll be military experts who advise them
under these circumstances, not rhetoricians.* What
are your thoughts about this, Gorgias? I mean, you're
a rhetorician, you say, and you train others to be
rhetoricians too, so it would be good to hear what
you have to say about your own area of expertise.
You should bear in mind our present situation and
realize that I have your best interests at heart. It's
quite possible that there are people here in the house
with us who'd like to become students of yours
... yes, I can see a few candidates—well, quite a lot,
in fact. They might be too embarrassed to subject
you to questioning, so as I put my questions, you
d should imagine that it's actually they who are asking
you, 'What will attending your courses hold for us,
Gorgias? What will we be able to advise Athens on?
Only matters of right and wrong, or the subjects
Socrates mentioned just now as well?' What do you
have to say in reply?

GORGIAS: All right, Socrates. I'll do my best to demonstrate what rhetoric is capable of doing and leave
nothing unclear. You cued me in perfectly yourself.
I mean, I assume you're aware that it was either
e Themistocles or Pericles, not the professionals, whose

18

advice led to those dockyards you mentioned, and to Athens' fortifications and the construction of the harbours.

SOCRATES: Yes, Gorgias. I only have it on hearsay about Themistocles, but I was there in person when Pericles advised us to build the Middle Wall.*

GORGIAS: And you can see, Socrates, that whenever 456a there's a decision to be made about any of the matters you mentioned just now, it's the rhetoricians whose suggestions are heard and whose opinions prevail.

SOCRATES: I find that incredible, Gorgias, and that's why I've been asking you all this time what rhetoric is capable of. Faced with phenomena like the one you've mentioned, it comes across as something supernatural, with enormous power.

GORGIAS: You don't know the half of it, Socrates! Almost every accomplishment falls within the scope of rhetoric. I've got good evidence of this. Often in the b past, when I've gone with my brother or some other doctor to one of their patients who was refusing to take his medicine or to let the doctor operate on him or cauterize him, the doctor proved incapable of persuading the patient to accept his treatment, but I succeeded, even though I didn't have any other expertise to draw on except rhetoric. Think of a community—any community you like—and I assure you that if an expert in rhetoric and a doctor went there and had to compete against each other for election as that community's doctor by addressing the Assembly or some other public meeting, the doctor would be left standing, and the effective speaker would win the c election, if that's what he wanted. In fact, it doesn't matter what his rival's profession is: the rhetorician would persuade them to choose him, and the other person would fail. It's inconceivable that a professional of any stamp could speak more persuasively in front of a crowd than a rhetorician on any topic at all.

19

So you can see how effective rhetoric is, and the kinds of things it's capable of doing. All the same, it should be used just as one would any other com- petitive skill. The fact that a person has trained as a
d boxer or a pancratiast* or a soldier, and can con- sequently defeat friends and enemies alike, doesn't mean he has to use this skill of his against everyone indiscriminately; it doesn't give him a reason to go around beating his friends up or stabbing them to death! Moreover, if someone goes to a gym, gets fit, and learns how to box, and then beats up his parents or some other friend or relation of his, this is certainly no reason for people to bear a grudge against trainers
e and people who teach others how to fight in armour, and ban them from their communities. A teacher passes his expertise on for his pupils to use when it is morally appropriate to do so—which is to say, defensively, not aggressively, and against people who wish them harm and do them wrong. It is the pupils
457a who corrupt and abuse their strength and their skills. This doesn't mean that the teachers are bad, and it doesn't mean that the expertise is at fault or is bad either; it only reflects on those who abuse it, surely.

The same goes for rhetoric. A rhetorician is cap- able of speaking effectively against all comers, whatever the issue, and can consequently be more persuasive in front of crowds about—to cut a long
b story short—anything he likes. Nevertheless, the fact that he's capable of getting people to think less highly of doctors and their fellow professionals doesn't mean that he has to do so. Just like any competitive skill, rhetoric should be used when morally appropriate. If a person becomes good at rhetoric and then uses the power this expertise brings to do wrong, surely people shouldn't bear a grudge against the teacher and ban him from their communities. He passed his
c expertise on for moral usage, and it's this pupil of his who's using it for the opposite reasons. Hostility, banishment, and execution may be fair responses to

20

abuse of rhetoric, but it's unfair to treat the teacher like that.

Before beginning to criticize what Gorgias has said about rhetoric, Socrates delivers a pointed warning against taking such arguments personally.

SOCRATES: There's a particular phenomenon that crops up during discussions, Gorgias, and you've experienced so many of them, like me, that I'm sure you've noticed it. People find it difficult to agree on exactly what it is they're trying to talk about, and this makes it hard for them to learn from one another and so bring their conversations to a mutually satisfactory conclusion. What happens instead, when two people d are arguing about something, is that one person tells the other that he's wrong or has expressed himself obscurely, and then they get angry and each thinks that his own point of view is being maliciously misinterpreted by the other person, and they start trying to win the argument rather than look into the issue they set out to discuss. Sometimes the argument finally breaks up in an appalling state, with people hurling abuse and saying the kinds of things to each other which can only make the bystanders cross at themselves for having thought these people worth listening to. e

You're probably wondering why I've brought this up. It's because I think that what you're saying now about rhetoric is incompatible and inconsistent to a certain extent with what you originally said. So I'm worried about subjecting your views to a thorough examination, in case you assume that the target of my argumentativeness is you, when all I really want to do is clarify the facts of the matter. If you're the same kind of person as I am, I'd be glad to continue 458a questioning you; otherwise, let's forget it. What kind of person am I? I'm happy to have a mistaken idea of mine proved wrong, and I'm happy to prove someone else's mistaken ideas wrong, I'm certainly

not *less* happy if I'm proved wrong than if I've proved someone else wrong, because, as I see it, I've got the best of it: there's nothing worse than the state which I've been saved from, so that's better for me than saving someone else. You see, there's nothing worse for a person, in my opinion, than holding mistaken views about the matters we're discussing at the
b moment.* Anyway, if you tell me that you and I are alike in this respect, then let's carry on talking; but if you think we'd better forget it, then let's do so and call a halt to the discussion right now.

GORGIAS: But I am like that, Socrates, I promise. Your description fits me perfectly. Still, perhaps we ought to think about the others here as well. Remember, I put on an extensive presentation for them, and that was quite a while ago—even before you and Chaerephon arrived. And now it's conceivable that our discussion might go on for rather a long time, so
c we ought to consider them too, in case we're keeping some of them from doing something else they want to do.

CHAEREPHON: You can hear from the noise people here are making, Gorgias and Socrates, that they want to hear whatever you have to say. As for me, I hope I'm never so busy that I have something to do which takes priority over a discussion as good and as well argued as this one, and makes me miss it.

d CALLICLES: I couldn't agree more, Chaerephon. I should think I've heard as many discussions in the past as you two, but I can't remember when I've enjoyed one as much as yours. I'd be delighted even if you wanted to go on talking all day long.

SOCRATES: Well, that's perfectly fine with me, Callicles, as long as Gorgias is happy.

GORGIAS: When all's said and done, Socrates, it would be embarrassing for *me* to refuse, since I claimed to be able to answer any questions which were put to
e me. If that's what they want, let's talk. You can ask me any questions you like.

22

Gorgias is in effect claiming, Socrates points out, that a rhetorician is a mere amateur who happens to know how to be more persuasive than a professional in front of other amateurs. Gorgias boldly grasps the nettle and insists that it is precisely the strength of rhetoric that it is all one needs to be a match for any other professional. However, he continues to claim that a rhetorician is also an expert in morality, and that he himself can teach others to be moral experts. Socrates argues that a moral expert must behave morally, as well as know about morality, and if so, then this contradicts Gorgias' earlier claim that rhetoricians can make immoral use of their expertise.

SOCRATES: All right, Gorgias, I'll tell you the problem I had with what you said. I mean, it's quite possible that what you were saying was right and I simply misunderstood you. You claim to be able to train up as a rhetorician anyone who's prepared to listen to your teaching on the subject. Yes?

GORGIAS: Yes.

SOCRATES: And you'll teach him all he needs to know to persuade a crowd of people—not to make them understand the issues, but to win them over. Is that right?

GORGIAS: Yes.

459a

SOCRATES: Now, you claimed a while back that a rhetorician would be more persuasive than a doctor even when the issue was health.

GORGIAS: Yes, I did, as long as he's speaking in front of a crowd.

SOCRATES: By 'in front of a crowd' you mean 'in front of non-experts', don't you? I mean, a rhetorician wouldn't be more persuasive than a doctor in front of an audience of experts, of course.

GORGIAS: True.

SOCRATES: Now, if he's more persuasive than a doctor, he's more persuasive than an expert, isn't he?

GORGIAS: Yes.

SOCRATES: When he isn't actually a doctor himself. Yes? b

GORGIAS: Yes.

SOCRATES: And a person who isn't a doctor is ignorant, of course, about the things which a doctor knows.

GORGIAS: Obviously.

SOCRATES: So any case of a rhetorician being more persuasive than a doctor is a case of a non-expert being more persuasive than an expert in front of an audience of non-experts. Isn't that what we have to conclude?

GORGIAS: Yes, in this instance, anyway.

SOCRATES: But isn't a practitioner of rhetoric in the same situation whatever the area of expertise? He never has to know the actual facts of any issue; instead,
c he's equipped himself with a persuasive ploy which enables him to make non-experts believe that he knows more than experts.*

GORGIAS: Doesn't that simplify things, Socrates? Rhetoric is the only area of expertise you need to learn. You can ignore all the rest and still get the better of the professionals!

SOCRATES: Let's leave the question of whether or not this means that a rhetorician does get the better of others, and look into it a little later, if it's relevant to our discussion. For the time being, however, we've got a prior question to investigate: is the rhetorician's situation actually the same with respect to
d right and wrong, morality and immorality, and good and bad, as it is with health and all the other provinces of particular areas of expertise? That is, despite lacking expert knowledge of good or bad, morality or immorality, or right or wrong, has he equipped himself with a persuasive ploy which enables him to make non-experts think that he's more of an expert than an expert, even though he isn't? Or does he
e have to be an expert? Is knowledge of these matters actually a prerequisite for someone to come and learn rhetoric from you? If it isn't, can you still (in your capacity as a teacher of rhetoric) give someone who comes to you the ability to make the general run of

24

people think he's an expert on morality when he isn't, and think he's a moral person when he isn't? I mean, I know it's not your job to bring anyone to understand any of these matters.* Or is it completely impossible for you to teach anyone rhetoric unless he already knows what is and is not the case in the sphere of morality? How do things stand here, Gorgias? And do please, I beg you, keep your recent 460a promise and demonstrate what rhetoric is capable of doing.*

GORGIAS: In my opinion, Socrates, he'll also learn about morality from me, if he really doesn't already know.*

SOCRATES: Stop there! I'm glad to hear you say that. So if you're to train someone as a rhetorician, he must either understand right and wrong beforehand, or gain this understanding at a later stage under your direction.

GORGIAS: Yes.

SOCRATES: Now, isn't a person who's come to under- b stand building a builder?

GORGIAS: Yes.

SOCRATES: While a person who's come to understand music is a musician. Yes?

GORGIAS: Yes.

SOCRATES: And a person who's come to understand medicine is a doctor, and so on and so forth. By the same token, anyone who has come to understand a given subject is described in accordance with the particular character his branch of knowledge confers. Do you agree?

GORGIAS: Yes.

SOCRATES: So doesn't it follow that someone who has come to understand morality is moral?

GORGIAS: Definitely. No doubt about it.*

SOCRATES: A moral person behaves morally, of course.

GORGIAS: Yes.

SOCRATES: A rhetorician is bound to be moral, then, c and a moral person is bound to want to behave morally. Agreed?

25

GORGIAS: I suppose so.

SOCRATES: So a rhetorician will never deliberately do wrong.

GORGIAS: Apparently not.

SOCRATES: Well, I'd like to remind you of something
d you said not long ago. You said that communities shouldn't hold trainers responsible and banish them for what a boxer does with his boxing—that is, for any wrongs he commits—and that by the same token it isn't the teacher who should be blamed or banned if a rhetorician uses his rhetoric for immoral purposes, but the person who is actually using rhetoric wrongly and incorrectly. Isn't that what you said?

GORGIAS: Yes, it is.

SOCRATES: But now it turns out that a rhetorician—the
e very person you were talking about—can *never* do wrong. Is that right?

GORGIAS: I suppose so.

SOCRATES: In fact, Gorgias, you know when you said earlier that the province of rhetoric was the spoken word in the field of right and wrong, rather than things like numerical oddness and evenness?

GORGIAS: Yes.

SOCRATES: Well, even then I took the implication of what you were saying to be that rhetoric could never be an immoral business, since morality is all it ever talks about. That was why I was astonished at the suggestion you made a little later that a rhetorician might
461a actually put his rhetoric to immoral use; I thought you were being inconsistent and so I said what I said about how our discussion would be worth while if you were like me and saw the profit in being proved wrong, but that otherwise we should just forget it. And now we've reached a point in our enquiry where you can see for yourself that we've come to the opposite conclusion—that a rhetorician is incapable of putting his rhetoric to immoral use and of deliberately doing wrong. I tell you, Gorgias, it's going to

take quite a lot of discussion to sort out the truth of these matters to our satisfaction. b

Gorgias' pupil Polus now takes over the discussion with Socrates. He complains that Socrates has exploited Gorgias' sense of propriety in order to win the argument and asks Socrates what he himself thinks rhetoric is. Socrates says that it is a kind of empirical knack, like cookery, and doesn't require technical expertise as such. Moreover, both rhetoric and cookery are aspects of 'flattery'—which is to say that they aim solely to give pleasure, rather than any genuine benefit. All branches of flattery are counterfeit imitations of true branches of knowledge. Four branches of flattery are schematically compared with their non-spurious counterparts.

POLUS: Come off it, Socrates. Do you actually believe what you've been saying about rhetoric? Do you think . . . just because Gorgias was too embarrassed not to accept the idea you introduced (that a rhetorical expert knows what is right, moral, and good, and that if a pupil didn't have this knowledge when he came to him, he'd teach him), and just because— as a result of this concession, I suppose*—there then turned out to be a degree of inconsistency in what he was saying, which is a situation you relish, when it c was you yourself who had steered him towards these questions . . . I mean, do you expect *anyone* to deny that he knows what's right and can explain it to other people? It's really rude of you to steer the discussion in that direction.

SOCRATES: My dear Polus, that's exactly why we've got friends and children, so that when we grow old and tottery, you younger ones are there to set our lives straight and correct any mistakes we make in our behaviour and our words. At the moment, you're the one who's here: if Gorgias and I have slipped up in d anything we've said, it's your duty to set us straight. I'll gladly take back anything you like—any of our conclusions which strikes you as wrong—just so long as you comply with one condition.

POLUS: What's that?

SOCRATES: At the beginning of this discussion,* you showed signs of wanting to express yourself in a long-winded fashion. Please could you restrain yourself on that score.

POLUS: What? Won't you let me speak at any length I choose?

e SOCRATES: Polus, it would certainly be dreadful for you to come here to Athens, where there's greater freedom of speech than anywhere else in Greece, and then to be the only person to be denied that opportunity. 'But look at it from the other point of view':* if you'd rather make long speeches than answer questions, wouldn't *I* be the one in trouble—unless I could just leave and avoid listening to you?

462a No, if you feel anything for the discussion you've just heard and would like to set it straight, you're welcome to take back any part of it, but then please do what Gorgias and I did: test me and let yourself be tested as well, by asking and answering questions. I mean, I imagine you claim to have the same accomplishments as Gorgias, don't you?

POLUS: Yes.

SOCRATES: In that case, do you too tell people from time to time to ask you any question they like, on the grounds that you'll know what answer to give?

POLUS: Yes.

b SOCRATES: So now please either ask questions or answer them, whichever you like.

POLUS: All right, here's a question for you, Socrates. According to you, Gorgias is unclear about rhetoric; so why don't you tell us what *you* think it is?

SOCRATES: Are you asking me what kind of expertise I think it is?

POLUS: Yes.

SOCRATES: To be perfectly frank, Polus, I don't think there's any expertise involved.

POLUS: Well, what do you think rhetoric is, then?

SOCRATES: Something which, according to an essay of yours I recently read,* is responsible for expertise. c

POLUS: What do you mean?

SOCRATES: I think it's a kind of experiential knack.*

POLUS: So that's what you think rhetoric is, do you?

SOCRATES: I do, unless you tell me otherwise.

POLUS: A knack at what?

SOCRATES: At producing pleasure and gratification.

POLUS: Wouldn't you say that the ability of rhetoric to please people is precisely what makes it so admirable?

SOCRATES: Polus, surely it's a secondary question whether I think rhetoric is admirable. You can only ask me that once you've found out from me what I think d rhetoric is. Have you done that?

POLUS: Yes, because you've told me you think it's a kind of knack.

SOCRATES: Well, since you're so keen on gratification, will you do me a small favour?

POLUS: Certainly.

SOCRATES: Ask me what kind of expertise I think cookery is.

POLUS: Okay. What kind of expertise is cookery?

SOCRATES: It isn't one at all, Polus. Go on, ask me why.

POLUS: All right, I do.

SOCRATES: It's a kind of knack. Ask me what it's a knack at.

POLUS: Yes, please tell us.

SOCRATES: At producing pleasure and gratification, Polus. e

POLUS: So cookery's the same as rhetoric?

SOCRATES: Of course not. It's just that it's a branch of the same activity.

POLUS: What activity?

SOCRATES: I don't want Gorgias to think I'm mocking what he does, so I'm a bit worried about speaking, in case the truth sounds rather rude. It's true that I'm not sure whether what I'm going to say *does* apply to rhetoric as Gorgias practises it, because in our 463a

29

recent discussion he didn't actually explain what he thought about rhetoric; but there's nothing admirable about the activity one of whose branches is what *I* call rhetoric.

GORGIAS: What activity is that, Socrates? Go on, you can tell us. You needn't feel embarrassed because of me.

SOCRATES: Well, in my opinion, Gorgias, it doesn't involve expertise; all you need is a mind which is good at guessing, some courage, and a natural talent for interacting with people. The general term I use to refer to it is 'flattery', and this strikes me as a multi-faceted activity, one of whose branches is cookery. And what I'm saying about cookery is that it does seem to be a branch of expertise, but in fact isn't: it's a knack, acquired by habituation. Another branch of the same activity is rhetoric, to my mind—and then there's ornamentation and sophistry as well. Each of these four branches has its own sphere of activity. I'd welcome any questions from Polus about this, because I haven't yet told him what particular kind of branch of flattery I think rhetoric is—not that it seems to matter to him that I haven't yet answered this question: he's already asking me whether I think rhetoric is an admirable activity. But I refuse to tell him whether I think rhetoric is admirable or contemptible before I've told him what it is. I'd be wrong to do so, Polus. So if you want to hear what I have to say, you'd better ask me what kind of branch of flattery I think rhetoric is.

POLUS: All right. Tell us what kind it is.

SOCRATES: I wonder if you'll understand the implications of my answer, though. In my opinion, you see, rhetoric is a phantom of a branch of statesmanship.

POLUS: Good. Now, do you think it's admirable or contemptible?

SOCRATES: Anything bad is contemptible, so in my opinion rhetoric is contemptible. But this answer of mine assumes that you understand what I'm getting at.

30

GORGIAS: Well, I have to tell you, Socrates, that *I* certainly don't understand what you're getting at.

SOCRATES: Why should you, Gorgias? I haven't yet made e my meaning plain. But our friend Polus here is young and impatient.*

GORGIAS: Well, never mind him. Why don't you tell *me* what you mean by saying that rhetoric is a phantom of a branch of statesmanship?

SOCRATES: All right. I'll try to explain what I think rhetoric is, and then Polus here will prove me wrong if my ideas turn out to be misguided. There's something you call 'body', isn't there, and something else you call 'mind'?

GORGIAS: Naturally.   464a

SOCRATES: And in the case of both the body and the mind, there's a state which is a state of health, wouldn't you say?

GORGIAS: Yes.

SOCRATES: Do you also think there's a state which only appears to be healthy, but isn't really? Here's the kind of situation I'm thinking of. It's quite common for people to seem to be physically healthy, and for no one except a doctor or a trainer to see that they actually aren't.

GORGIAS: You're right.

SOCRATES: In my opinion, this is a mental phenomenon as well. I think the mind as well as the body can be in the kind of condition which makes it seem to be in a good state when it really isn't at all.

GORGIAS: True.   b

SOCRATES: All right, now I'll explain my position better, if I can. In my opinion, there are two areas of expertise, corresponding to these two domains. I call the area of expertise whose province is the mind 'statesmanship'; I can't quite find a single term to apply to the one whose province is the body, but I'd say that looking after the body is a single area of expertise and that it has two branches, exercise and medicine. Within statesmanship, the legislative

31

process corresponds to exercise and the administration of justice to medicine.* Because they're concerned
c with the same province, there's some overlap between them—between medicine and exercise on the one hand, and the administration of justice and the legislative process on the other—but there are also differences.

There are these four branches of expertise, then, and all they ever aim for is what's best for the body or the mind, whichever it is they look after. Flattery noticed them—guessed their natures, I should say, rather than understood them—and divided herself into four. She can impersonate each of the four branches of expertise and make herself out to be any of them, whichever one's persona she takes on. She
d isn't interested in the slightest in the best course of action, but she traps and deceives foolish people with the promise of maximizing immediate pleasure, which makes her seem better than any alternative. Cookery impersonates medicine, for instance, and pretends to know what food is best for the body;* so if children (or adults with as little intelligence as children) were judging a contest between a cook and a doctor as to which of them—the doctor or the cook—was the
e expert on the subject of good and bad food, they'd sentence the doctor to death by starvation!*

I call cookery a kind of flattery, then, and I maintain
465a that it's contemptible—this point is addressed to you, Polus—because its aim is pleasure rather than welfare. But I don't think it's an area of expertise: I think it's a knack, because it lacks rational understanding either of the object of its attentions or of the nature of the things it dispenses (and so it can't explain the reason why anything happens), and it's inconceivable to me that anything irrational involves expertise. If you dispute any of this, I'd be happy to submit it to a reasoned argument.

b So cookery, as I say, is the counterpart within flattery of medicine. By the same token, ornamentation

32

is the counterpart of exercise, in the sense that it is fraudulent, deceitful, petty, and servile. It misleadingly alters a person's shape and complexion; it makes his skin all smooth and dresses him up. And so it enables people to take on a beauty which is not their own and to disregard their own innate attractions, which can be developed through exercise. To help me to be brief, and because I think you'll understand me now, I want to say (at the risk of sounding like a mathematician) that as ornamentation is to exer- c cise, so cookery is to medicine—or rather, as ornamentation is to exercise, so sophistry is to the legislative process, and as cookery is to medicine, so rhetoric is to the administration of justice.

Although sophistry and rhetoric are essentially different, in the way I've described, there are, as I say,* enough similarities for their practitioners to find themselves all jumbled together in the same province and with the same concerns, until they don't know what to make of one another and no one else does either. In fact, if the body were self-regulating and didn't have the mind to control it (in other words, if d the mind didn't take a good look at cookery and medicine and conclude that they're different, but the body drew its own conclusions on the basis of its own feelings of pleasure), then the situation Anaxagoras describes—I'm sure you know what I'm talking about, my dear Polus—would be rife:* everything would be jumbled up together, with no differentiation between the practices of medicine and healing and those of cookery.

So now you know what I think about rhetoric. It corresponds to cookery: as cookery is to the body, e so rhetoric is to the mind. You might think that my behaviour has been ridiculous: first I stopped you making long speeches and now I've gone on for so long myself. Well, I think you should forgive me, because when I kept my answers brief, you didn't understand me and completely failed to cope with

466a   what I was saying. If I can't cope with your answers
         either, *you* can develop what you want to say at
         length as well; if I can, though, you mustn't stop me
         doing so. That's fair for both of us. So if there's any
         response you want to make now to the position I've
         stated, please go ahead.

*Polus is surprised at Socrates' belittlement of rhetoric,
because political speakers surely have power. Astonishingly, and boldly, Socrates denies this. In an argument
which is perhaps too subtle for its own good, he claims
that the ability to do what seems best does not necessarily imply the ability to do what you actually want,
since what you actually want at any time is what is
good for you, and although like everyone else politicians always aim for their own good, they may fail to
realize where their own good lies, and so not do what
they want. Politicians, Socrates implies, are more likely
than others to decide to follow others' whims—to pan-
der to the populace, for instance—rather than pursue
their own good, and therefore, paradoxically, those who
apparently have the most power have the least.*

POLUS: So, in your opinion, to be a rhetorician is to be
    a flatterer, is it? Is that what you're saying?
SOCRATES: Well, what I actually said was that rhetoric
    was a *branch* of flattery.* So young, and yet so for-
    getful, Polus! It makes me wonder what you'll be like
    before long.
POLUS: So you think people have a low opinion of good
    rhetoricians, do you? Their fellow citizens consider
    them flatterers, you say?
b SOCRATES: Is this a genuine question or the beginning of
    a speech?
POLUS: A genuine question.
SOCRATES: I myself don't think people have any opinion
    at all about them.
POLUS: But of course they do! Rhetoricians are the
    most powerful members of their communities, aren't
    they?*

34

SOCRATES: No, not if you believe that power is a good thing for its possessor.

POLUS: I most certainly do believe that.

SOCRATES: Well, I think rhetoricians are the *least* powerful members of a community.

POLUS: What? Don't they resemble dictators in that they can execute anyone they want, and confiscate a person's property and then banish that person from their community if it seems best?

SOCRATES: Honestly, Polus, I just can't make up my mind whether you really mean anything you say and are expressing your own opinion, or are simply asking me for my views about it.

POLUS: Well, I'm certainly asking you what you think.

SOCRATES: All right, my friend. In that case, you're asking me two questions at the same time, aren't you?

POLUS: What do you mean?

SOCRATES: Didn't you just say, 'Don't rhetoricians resemble dictators in that they can execute anyone they want, and can confiscate a person's property and then drive that person out of their communities if it seems best?'?

POLUS: I did.

SOCRATES: Well, I'd say there are two questions here. Here's my response to them both. In my opinion, Polus—and this is to repeat what I said a moment ago—rhetoricians and dictators are the least powerful members of their communities, because they almost never do what they want, rather than what they think it's best for them to do.

POLUS: But isn't this what it is to have a great deal of power?

SOCRATES: No, not according to Polus.

POLUS: Not according to me? But I *do* think so.

SOCRATES: I assure you that . . . No, you don't, since you claim that a great deal of power is a good thing for its possessor.

POLUS: Yes, I do claim that.

SOCRATES: Well, suppose an unintelligent person does

what he thinks it's best for him to do—is that a good thing, do you think? Would you describe this as an instance of great power?

POLUS: No, I wouldn't.

SOCRATES: So why don't you prove me wrong by demonstrating that rhetoricians aren't unintelligent—in other words, that rhetoric is an area of expertise, not a kind of flattery?* As long as this claim of mine remains in place, any rhetoricians who do what they think it's best for them to do in their communities won't benefit at all from this, and the same goes for dictators too. Power is a good thing, according to you, but you agree with me that action based on unwise decisions is a bad thing. Yes?

POLUS: Yes.

SOCRATES: Why should we suppose, then, that rhetoricians or dictators have a great deal of power in their communities? Polus would have to prove Socrates wrong and demonstrate that rhetoricians and dictators do what they *want*.

POLUS: Just listen to him! He . . .

SOCRATES: I'm denying that they do what they want. Can you prove me wrong?

POLUS: Didn't you concede a short while ago that they do what they think it's best for them to do?

SOCRATES: Yes, I agree with that.

POLUS: Aren't they doing what they want, then?

SOCRATES: No, I don't think so.

POLUS: Even though they're doing what they think it's best to do?

SOCRATES: Yes.

POLUS: You're really being extraordinarily obstinate, Socrates.

SOCRATES: Please don't be rude, peerless Polus—look, this salutation of mine sounds like something you might have said!* Either prove me wrong, if you've got any questions to ask me, or else let me ask you some questions.

POLUS: I don't mind if you ask the questions,

because it'll help me understand what you're getting at.

SOCRATES: Tell me, then, do you think people want whatever it is they're doing on any given occasion, or do they want whatever it is that what they're doing is a means towards? For example, when people drink medicine which a doctor has given them, do you think their objective is what they're doing—that is, drinking the medicine and suffering*—or that thing (in this case health) which the drinking of the medicine is a means towards?

POLUS: Obviously it's health.

SOCRATES: What about businessmen, then, when they d make a sea voyage or whatever? Again, they don't want what they're doing at the time—who could possibly *want* all the risks of a sea voyage and all the bother that commerce brings? What they want is what the voyage is a means towards, in this case wealth. Wealth is the reason they make sea voyages.

POLUS: Yes.

SOCRATES: In fact, isn't it a universal principle that whenever someone does one thing for the sake of another thing, what he wants is not what he's actually doing, but whatever it is that what he's doing is a means towards?

POLUS: Yes.

SOCRATES: Now, isn't everything in the world either e good, bad, or indifferent (which is to say, neither good nor bad)?

POLUS: That's absolutely inevitable, Socrates.

SOCRATES: And would you count knowledge, health, wealth, and so on as good, and their opposites as bad?

POLUS: Yes.

SOCRATES: What about 'neither good nor bad'? Do you think this description fits things which sometimes take on the quality of being good and sometimes that of being bad, and at other times are neutral? I mean things like sitting, walking, running, and sailing, for 468a instance, or again things like stones, sticks, and so on. What do you think? Are these the kinds of things you'd describe as neither good nor bad, or would you keep that description for other things?

POLUS: No, I'd apply it to the things you've mentioned.

SOCRATES: Now, do people invariably use these neutral activities as a way of getting good things, or do they use good things as a way of getting indifferent things?

POLUS: They use neutral activities as a way of getting good things, of course.

b SOCRATES: Walking, then, is something we do because we want good* and we think walking is better on that occasion than not walking. Conversely we stay where we are, when we do so, in pursuit of the same thing—that is, good. Yes?

POLUS: Yes.

SOCRATES: Suppose we execute somebody, then, or exile him or confiscate his property. Is this another class of actions we perform because it seems better for us to do them than not to do them?

POLUS: Yes.

SOCRATES: People do all the things I've mentioned, then, in pursuit of good.

POLUS: I agree.

SOCRATES: And haven't we agreed that whenever we do one thing for the sake of another thing, what we want is not what we're actually doing, but whatever

c it is that what we're doing is a means towards?

POLUS: We certainly have.

SOCRATES: We don't, then, in an unqualified sense, *want* to slaughter people or exile them from their communities or confiscate their property. We *want* to do these things only if they're in our interest, but if they're not we don't want to do them because, as you admit, we want good things, but don't want things which are either indifferent or bad. Yes? . . . Do you think I'm right or not, Polus? . . . Why aren't you replying?

POLUS: Yes, you're right.

d SOCRATES: Well, bearing in mind this conclusion of ours,

38

let's consider the case of someone—he may be a dictator or a rhetorician—who executes another person or banishes him or confiscates his property, in the belief that it's better for him to do so, when in fact it's worse. He's doing what he thinks it's best for him to do, isn't he?

POLUS: Yes.

SOCRATES: Well, given that what he's doing is in fact bad for him, is he also doing what he wants? . . . Why aren't you answering my question?

POLUS: All right. I agree that he isn't doing what he wants.*

SOCRATES: How can a person in this position possibly have a great deal of power in his community, then, e given that according to you a great deal of power is a good thing?

POLUS: He can't.

SOCRATES: I was right, then, when I said that someone might do what he thinks it's best for him to do in his community, but still fail to have a great deal of power and fail to do what he wants.*

In response to Polus' ad hominem retort that Socrates must find holding others' lives in one's hands enviable, Socrates not only denies this, but pulls the rug out from under Polus' feet by adding that it is better to suffer wrong than to do it. Wrongdoing is always pitiable; true profit and happiness lie in being morally good. Polus regards this as nonsense and cites the case of Archelaus, an autocrat who was commonly held to be happy, but Socrates is unimpressed. He requires sound argument, not rhetoric, to convince him, especially about issues as important as the nature of happiness.

POLUS: As if you wouldn't prefer to be able to do whatever you felt like doing in your community rather than the opposite, Socrates! You make it sound as though the sight of someone executing people when he thinks it's best, or confiscating their property, or throwing them into prison, doesn't make you envious.

SOCRATES: Do you mean when these actions of his are justified or when they're unjustified?

469a POLUS: It doesn't make any difference. Isn't it enviable anyway?

SOCRATES: That's a terrible thing to say, Polus.

POLUS: Why?

SOCRATES: Because pity, not envy, is the appropriate response to people who are either unenviable or unhappy.

POLUS: Do you really think these descriptions fit the people I've been talking about?

SOCRATES: Of course they do.

POLUS: Well, if a person decides to execute someone, and does so, and is *right* to have done so, is he unhappy or in a pitiful state, do you think?

SOCRATES: No, I don't, but he's certainly not in an enviable position.

POLUS: But didn't you just claim that he was unhappy?

b SOCRATES: No, Polus, I meant that anyone who executes a person *un*justly is in an unhappy state, and deserves our pity as well; to do so justly is merely unenviable.

POLUS: Well, at least it's certain that the person who's being wrongly executed is in a pitiful and unhappy state!

SOCRATES: But less so than his executioner, Polus, and less so than a person whose execution is just.

POLUS: What do you mean, Socrates?

SOCRATES: I mean that in actual fact there's nothing worse than doing wrong.

POLUS: Really? *Nothing* worse? Isn't it worse to suffer wrong?

SOCRATES: No, not at all.

POLUS: So you'd rather have wrong done to you than do wrong?

c SOCRATES: I'd rather avoid them both, but if I had to choose between doing wrong and having wrong done to me, I'd prefer the latter to the former.

POLUS: So you wouldn't opt for being a dictator?

40

SOCRATES: No, if dictatorship means the same to you as it does to me.

POLUS: What I mean by it is what I said a moment ago, the licence to do whatever you think it's best for you to do in your community—the licence to execute people and banish them, and to go to any lengths to see your personal predilections fulfilled.

SOCRATES: Well, Polus, here are some thoughts of *mine* for you to criticize. Imagine I'm in the agora when d it's chock-full, and I've got a dagger tucked in my armpit.* I tell you, 'Polus, I've recently gained an incredible amount of power, as much as any dictator. Look at all these people. If I decide one of them has to die, he's dead, just like that; if I decide one of them should have his head split open, it'll be split open on the spot; if I decide someone's cloak needs shredding, shredded it is. So you can see that I have e a great deal of power in this community.' And suppose you don't believe me, so I show you my dagger. I bet you'd say, 'Socrates, in that case everyone has a great deal of power, since by the same token you could also burn down any houses you decide to burn down—and then there are Athens' dockyards and warships and the whole merchant fleet in public and private ownership.' So the ability to do what you feel like doing isn't a sign of a great deal of power. What do you think?

POLUS: I agree, it isn't. Not that kind of power, anyway.

SOCRATES: Can you tell us what's wrong with that sort 470a of power, to your mind?

POLUS: Yes.

SOCRATES: What is it? Do please tell us.

POLUS: It's that anyone who does the kinds of things you were describing is bound to be punished.   .

SOCRATES: By which you mean that punishment is bad?

POLUS: Yes.

SOCRATES: So you've again come round to the view, my friend, that doing what it seems best to do is a good thing if it turns out to be in one's interest to do it.

That, I suppose, is what it is to have a great deal of power. If it isn't in one's interest, however, it's a bad thing, and signifies little power. And here's another

b   point for us to consider. Are we agreed that the actions we were talking about a while back (the execution and banishment of people and the confiscation of property) may be better or worse, depending on the circumstances?

POLUS: Yes.

SOCRATES: Here's something we apparently both agree on, then!

POLUS: Yes.

SOCRATES: Well, what are the circumstances under which they become better, do you think? Can you tell me what makes the difference, in your opinion?

POLUS: I'd like to hear your response to that question, Socrates.

c   SOCRATES: You'd rather hear what I have to say? All right, Polus. My view is that if they're morally right, they're better, but if they're wrong, they're worse.

POLUS: Do you want to know how unassailable a position you're in, Socrates? Even a child could prove this idea of yours wrong.

SOCRATES: Then I'd be very grateful to the child. But I'll be no less grateful to you if you prove me wrong and free me from the snares of absurdity. You should never tire of doing friends favours, so go on: prove me wrong.

POLUS: Well, I don't need ancient history to help me prove you wrong, Socrates: there's enough counter-

d   evidence from the very recent past for me to show that happiness and wrongdoing do commonly go together.

SOCRATES: What is this evidence?

POLUS: You know that man Archelaus, Perdiccas' son, the one who rules Macedonia?*

SOCRATES: Not exactly, but I've heard of him.

POLUS: Does he strike you as being happy or unhappy?

SOCRATES: I don't know, Polus. I've never met the man.

POLUS: Would you really have to meet him before ap- e
preciating how happy he is? Can't you tell already?

SOCRATES: No, I certainly can't.

POLUS: It goes without saying that you won't admit that
the king of Persia is happy either,* Socrates.

SOCRATES: No, and I'm right not to, since I don't know
whether or not he's an educated, moral person.

POLUS: Does happiness really depend entirely on that?

SOCRATES: Yes, I think so, Polus. In my opinion, it takes
true goodness to make a man or a woman happy,*
and an immoral, wicked person is unhappy.

POLUS: My man Archelaus is unhappy, then, according 471a
to you.

SOCRATES: Yes, if he does wrong, Polus.

POLUS: But of course he does.* He didn't have the
slightest claim to the throne he currently occupies.
His mother was a slave of Perdiccas' brother Alcetas,
so by rights he should have been Alcetas' slave too.
If he'd wanted to behave morally, he'd have been
Alcetas' slave and that would have made him happy,
according to you. As it is, though, he's become incredibly unhappy as a result of the awful crimes he's
committed! In the first place, he sent a message to
Alcetas, who was his uncle as well as his master,* in b
which he invited him to stay on the grounds that he
would restore the kingdom which Perdiccas had
stolen from him. So he welcomed Alcetas and his
son Alexander, his own cousin (who was more or
less the same age as him), into his house; then he got
them drunk, bundled them into a cart, took them
away under cover of darkness, murdered them both,
and disposed of the bodies. He didn't realize how
terribly unhappy these crimes had made him and he
showed no sign of regret either, but a little later
made his next victim his brother, a lad aged about c
seven, who was Perdiccas' legitimate son and the
rightful heir to the throne. Instead of choosing
happiness by following the moral course of looking
after the lad until he had grown up and then handing

the kingdom over to him, he threw him into a well and drowned him—and then told the boy's mother Cleopatra that he'd fallen in and died while chasing a goose. There's no one in Macedonia, then, who has committed worse crimes than him, and that's why he's the most miserable Macedonian alive today, not the happiest. And that also explains why everyone in Athens would presumably follow your lead: Archelaus

d would be the last Macedonian they'd swap places with!

SOCRATES: I want to repeat a point I made early in our conversation,* Polus, when I complimented you on what I'm sure is an excellent training in rhetoric— but was disappointed to find that you've taken no interest in how to carry on a rational argument. Is the argument you've just come up with the one by means of which 'even a child' would expose my errors? Do you really think that with this argument you've disproved my claim that a criminal isn't happy? How on earth could you think that, my friend? I have to tell you that I disagree with absolutely everything you're saying.

e POLUS: You mean you're not prepared to admit it; you do actually agree with me.

SOCRATES: The trouble is, Polus, that you're trying to use on me the kind of rhetorical refutation which people in lawcourts think is successful. There too, you see, people think they're proving the other side wrong if they produce a large number of eminent witnesses in support of the points they're making, but their opponent comes up with only a single witness or none at all. This kind of refutation, how-ever, is completely worthless in the context of the

472a truth, since it's perfectly possible for someone to be defeated in court by a horde of witnesses with no more than apparent respectability who all testify falsely against him. In the present dispute, if you feel like calling witnesses to claim that what I'm saying is

44

wrong, you can count on your position being supported by almost everyone in Athens, whether they were born and bred here or elsewhere. You'd have the support of Nicias the son of Niceratus, if you wanted, along with his brothers, who between them have a whole row of tripods standing in the precinct of Dionysus.* You'd have the support of Aristocrates the son of Scellias as well, who has also made a b votive offering, in this case that wonderful one in the precinct of Pythian Apollo.* You could call on the whole of Pericles' household, if you felt like it, or any other Athenian family you care to choose.

Nevertheless, there's still a dissenting voice, albeit a single one—mine. You're producing no compelling reason why I should agree with you; all you're doing is calling up a horde of false witnesses against me to support your attempt to dislodge me from my inheritance, the truth.* To my mind, however, I won't have accomplished anything important with regard to the issues we've been discussing, unless I get you yourself to act as my witness—albeit a single one!— to testify to the truth of my position; and I'm sure c you won't think you've accomplished anything important either unless I testify for your position. It doesn't matter that there's only one of me; you'd let all the others go if you could get me as your witness.

So although there's the kind of refutation whose validity you take for granted (and you're far from being alone), there's also another kind, the kind I have in mind. Let's compare them and see how they differ. You see, the issues we're disagreeing about are in fact hardly trivial: I'd almost go so far as to say that in their case there's nothing more admirable than knowledge and nothing more contemptible than ignorance, since that would amount to knowledge or ignorance about what it is to be happy and what it is to be unhappy.

*Socrates states his two propositions: that a criminal is
bound to be unhappy, and that he will be more unhappy if he is not caught and punished. Polus is initially scornful, but Socrates gains his crucial admission
that wrongdoing is more contemptible than suffering wrong, and uses this admission to gain his
further admission that wrongdoing is actually disadvantageous to the wrongdoer. He leaves implicit the
conclusion that a criminal is therefore bound to be
unhappy.*

d SOCRATES: Let's start with the question facing us, which
is the crux of our present discussion. You think it's
possible for someone to be happy in spite of the fact
that he does wrong and is an immoral person, and
you cite the case of Archelaus who is, in your opinion, an immoral, but happy, person. Is that a fair
representation of your view?

POLUS: Yes.

SOCRATES: On the other hand, I claim that this is impossible. So here's one point on which we disagree. Now
then, this happy criminal . . . will he be happy if he
pays the penalty for his actions and is punished?

POLUS: Definitely not. That would make his condition
very unhappy.

e SOCRATES: So is it your view that a criminal is happy as
long as he doesn't get punished?

POLUS: Yes.

SOCRATES: My view, however, Polus, is that although
an unjust person, a criminal, is in a thoroughly
wretched state, he's worse off if he doesn't pay the
penalty and continues to do wrong without getting
punished than if he does pay the penalty and has
punishment meted out to him by gods and men.

473a POLUS: That's an extraordinary position to take, Socrates.

SOCRATES: And it's exactly the one I'm going to try to
convert you to as well, my friend—I do count you
as a friend, you see. Now, as things stand at the
moment, the difference between us is this. Please see

46

whether I've got this right. I maintained earlier* that doing wrong was worse than suffering wrong.

POLUS: Yes.

SOCRATES: While you claimed that suffering wrong was worse.

POLUS: Yes.

SOCRATES: And then my claim about the unhappiness of criminals was refuted by you ...

POLUS: It certainly was.

SOCRATES: Or so you think, Polus.   b

POLUS: And I'm right.

SOCRATES: Maybe, maybe not. Anyway, you then said that criminals were happy as long as they avoided punishment.

POLUS: That's right.

SOCRATES: Whereas my position is that this makes their condition completely wretched, and that punishment alleviates their condition somewhat. Do you want to refute this as well?

POLUS: It's going to be really hard to disprove this claim, Socrates—even harder than it was to refute the earlier one.*

SOCRATES: It's not just hard, Polus—it's impossible. The truth can never be proved wrong.*

POLUS: What do you mean? Imagine someone who's been caught in a criminal conspiracy against a dictatorship. After having been captured, he's stretched c on the rack, bits of his body are cut off, his eyes are burned out, and he's terribly mutilated in a great many and a wide variety of other ways; in addition to being mutilated himself, he watches his wife and children being tortured as well; finally he's crucified or covered with boiling pitch. Is this a happier state for him to be in than if he'd avoided being caught, had become dictator, and had spent the rest of his life ruling over his community and doing whatever he wanted, with everyone from home and abroad regarding him with envy and congratulating him for d his happiness? Is this your 'irrefutable' position?

47

SOCRATES: My dear Polus, first it was witnesses, now it's scare tactics. You're not doing anything to prove me wrong. Still, please refresh my memory a bit. The man in your scenario was involved in a criminal conspiracy against a dictatorship?

POLUS: Yes.

SOCRATES: Well then, neither situation will make him happier—whether he succeeds in making himself dictator by criminal means or pays the penalty—because you can't compare any two miserable people and say that one is happier than the other. Neverthe-

e   less, if he avoids being caught and becomes dictator, his stock of misery will increase. What's this, Polus? You're laughing? Is this yet another kind of refutation, which has you laughing at ideas rather than proving them wrong?

POLUS: Don't you think the sheer eccentricity of what you're saying is enough of a refutation, Socrates? Why don't you ask anyone here whether they agree with you?

SOCRATES: I'm no politician, Polus. In fact, last year I was on the Council, thanks to the lottery, and when it was the turn of my tribe to form the executive committee* and I had to put an issue to the vote, I

474a   made a fool of myself by not knowing the procedure for this. So please don't tell me to ask the present company to vote now either. No, if this is your best shot at a refutation, why don't you do what I suggested a short while ago* and let me have a go at one? Then you'll see what I think a refutation should be like. My expertise is restricted to producing just a single witness in support of my ideas—the person with whom I'm carrying on the discussion—and I pay no attention to large numbers of people; I only know how to ask for a single person's vote, and I can't even begin to address people in large groups.

b   What I'm wondering, then, is whether you'll be prepared to submit to an attempt at refutation by answering questions. You see, I think that both of us—and everyone else as well, in fact—believe that doing wrong is worse than suffering wrong, and that for a wrongdoer not paying the penalty is worse than doing so.

POLUS: And I say that no one—not me, and not anyone else either—believes that. Would *you* prefer to have wrong done to you than to do wrong?

SOCRATES: Yes, and so would you and everyone else.

POLUS: You're quite wrong. I wouldn't, you wouldn't, and nobody else would either.

SOCRATES: Why don't you answer my questions, then? c

POLUS: All right. I'm certainly longing to hear what you're going to say.

SOCRATES: You'll find out; you only have to answer my questions. I'll pretend that we're starting afresh. Which do you think is worse, Polus, doing wrong or having wrong done to you?

POLUS: Having wrong done to you, I'd say.

SOCRATES: And which is more contemptible, doing wrong or having wrong done to you? Can you tell me what you think?

POLUS: Doing wrong.

SOCRATES: Well, isn't it also worse, given that it's more contemptible?*

POLUS: Certainly not.

SOCRATES: I see. You don't identify 'admirable' with 'good', and 'contemptible' with 'bad', apparently.   d

POLUS: No, I don't.

SOCRATES: But what about this? Isn't there always a standard to which you refer before calling things admirable? It doesn't matter what the object is; it could be a body, a colour, a figure, a sound or an activity. Take an admirable physique, for instance. Don't you call it admirable either on account of its utility (by considering the particular purpose it is useful for), or on account of a certain kind of pleasure (if it gives people pleasure to look at it)? Can you think of anything else which might make one admire a person's physique?

49

e POLUS: No, I can't.

SOCRATES: And doesn't the same go for everything else as well? Don't you call figures and colours admirable either because they give a certain kind of pleasure, or because they're beneficial, or for both reasons at once?

POLUS: Yes.

SOCRATES: And isn't that also the case with sounds and all musical phenomena?

POLUS: Yes.

SOCRATES: And these criteria are surely relevant to the whole sphere of people's customs and activities as well. I mean, provided they're admirable, they're either beneficial or pleasant or both.

475a POLUS: I agree.

SOCRATES: And does the same go for admirable fields of study too?

POLUS: Yes. In fact, Socrates, in defining what is admirable in terms of pleasure and goodness, as you are at the moment, you've come up with an admirable definition!*

SOCRATES: And also if I define what is contemptible in the opposite way, in terms of unpleasantness and harmfulness?

POLUS: Yes, of course.

SOCRATES: So when one of a pair of admirable things is more admirable than the other, this is because it exceeds the other in one of these two respects or in both—either in pleasantness or in benefit or in both at once.

POLUS: Yes.

SOCRATES: And when one of a pair of contemptible things

b is more contemptible than the other, this is because it exceeds the other either in unpleasantness or in harmfulness. Isn't that bound to be so?

POLUS: Yes.

SOCRATES: Now, what was the position we reached a moment ago as regards doing and suffering wrong? Didn't you maintain that although suffering wrong was worse, doing it was more contemptible?

50

POLUS: Yes, I did.

SOCRATES: So if doing wrong is more contemptible than
suffering wrong, then either it's more unpleasant and
it's more contemptible because it exceeds the alternative in unpleasantness, or it's more contemptible
because it exceeds the alternative in harmfulness or
in both qualities at once. Isn't that bound to be the
case?

POLUS: Of course.

SOCRATES: So the first point for us to consider is whether c
doing wrong is more unpleasant than suffering wrong,
and whether people who do wrong are more dis-
tressed than those who have it done to them.

POLUS: No, of course that's not the case, Socrates.

SOCRATES: So it doesn't exceed the alternative in
unpleasantness.

POLUS: No.

SOCRATES: And if that's the case, it doesn't exceed the
alternative in *both* respects either.

POLUS: That seems right.

SOCRATES: The only remaining possibility, then, is that
it exceeds the alternative in the other respect.

POLUS: Yes.

SOCRATES: In harmfulness.

POLUS: I suppose so.

SOCRATES: Well, if doing wrong exceeds suffering wrong
in harmfulness, it must be worse than suffering
wrong.

POLUS: Obviously.

SOCRATES: Now, isn't it invariably accepted, and wasn't d
it admitted by you earlier, that doing wrong is more
contemptible than suffering wrong?

POLUS: Yes.

SOCRATES: And now we've found that it's worse as well.

POLUS: So it seems.

SOCRATES: Well, if *you* were faced with a choice between
two things, and one of them was worse and more
contemptible than the other, would you prefer it to
the alternative?* ... Don't you feel like answering?

You needn't worry: you won't come to any harm. Imagine that the argument is a doctor who demands sincerity from you, and tell us what you think. Do you say yes or no to my question?

e POLUS: No, I wouldn't prefer it, Socrates.

SOCRATES: Would anyone?

POLUS: I don't think so: the argument doesn't make it seem possible.

SOCRATES: I was right, then, when I suggested that doing wrong is held by everyone, including you and me, to be less preferable than suffering wrong, and the reason I was right is that doing wrong is in fact worse than having it done to you.

POLUS: I suppose so.

SOCRATES: Now that we've compared our techniques of refutation, Polus, you can see how completely different they are. You rely on the fact that everyone in the world agrees with you except for me, while I'm satisfied if I gain the assent of just one person—you.

476a I'm content if *you* testify to the validity of my argument, and I canvass only for your vote, without caring about what everyone else thinks.

Having proved to his satisfaction that doing wrong is universally held to be worse than suffering wrong, Socrates argues that it is better for an immoral person to be punished than to remain unpunished, just as it is better for a sick person to undergo medical treatment.

SOCRATES: So much for that issue. Next we need to look into the second point of disagreement between us. You claim that nothing could be worse for a criminal than paying the penalty for his crimes, whereas I claim that he's worse off if he doesn't pay the penalty. Which of us if right? Here's a way into the question: would you agree that there's no difference between a criminal paying the penalty for his crimes and being justly punished for them?

POLUS: Yes.

b SOCRATES: Now, wouldn't you describe any instance of

justice as admirable, in so far as it is just? Think about it. What's your view?

POLUS: I think it has to be admirable, Socrates.

SOCRATES: What about this, then? If a person does something, doesn't there also have to be something which undergoes what that person is doing?

POLUS: I think so.

SOCRATES: And isn't the object which is undergoing the action also bound to be affected by the *way* the agent acts? For instance, if a person hits, there must be something which is hit.

POLUS: Of course there must.

SOCRATES: And if the hitter hits hard or fast, it also follows that the object which is hit is hit in that way. c

POLUS: Yes.

SOCRATES: The effect on the object which is hit, then, is qualified by the way in which the hitter performs the action.

POLUS: Agreed.

SOCRATES: Then again, if a person cauterizes, there must be something which is cauterized, mustn't there?

POLUS: Of course.

SOCRATES: And if the process of cautery is intense or painful, the cauterized object is inevitably cauterized in the way in which the cautery is performed. Yes?

POLUS: Yes.

SOCRATES: And the same goes for when someone makes a cut, doesn't it? That is, something is cut.

POLUS: Yes.

SOCRATES: And if the incision is large or deep or painful, then isn't the cut object cut in a way which d reflects the kind of cut the cutter is making?

POLUS: Obviously.

SOCRATES: To sum up, then, do you agree with what I said a moment ago—that in all cases the affected object is affected in a way which reflects the way in which the agent acts?

POLUS: Yes, I agree.

SOCRATES: Please bear these conclusions in mind. I want

to ask next whether to be punished is to do something or to have something done to you.

POLUS: It's to have something done to you, of course, Socrates.

SOCRATES: And this something is done by an agent, presumably.

POLUS: Naturally. By the person who implements the punishment.

SOCRATES: And when a person is right to carry out a punishment, is he justified in doing so?

e POLUS: Yes.

SOCRATES: Is he acting justly, then, or not?

POLUS: He is.

SOCRATES: So to be punished by paying a fair penalty for your crimes is to have justice done to you?

POLUS: Obviously.

SOCRATES: But we've agreed that anything just is admirable, haven't we?

POLUS: Yes.

SOCRATES: So the agent is carrying out an admirable deed, while the one who's being punished is having an admirable deed done to him.

POLUS: Yes.

SOCRATES: Now, if he's having an admirable deed done
477a to him, he must be having a good deed done to him, in the sense that it's either pleasant or beneficial.

POLUS: Yes, he must be.

SOCRATES: Anyone who pays a fair penalty for his crimes, then, is having good done to him. Agreed?

POLUS: I suppose so.

SOCRATES: He's being benefited, then, isn't he?*

POLUS: Yes.

SOCRATES: I imagine that the kind of benefit he receives if his punishment is just is that his mind is made better. Do you think I'm right?

POLUS: It sounds plausible.

SOCRATES: If so, then a person who pays a fair penalty for his crimes is escaping a bad psychological state, isn't he?

POLUS: Yes.

SOCRATES: In which case, he's escaping the worst state there is, isn't he? Look at it this way: can you think b of anything other than poverty which constitutes a bad state for one's financial condition?

POLUS: No, that's it.

SOCRATES: What about a person's physical condition? Wouldn't you say that in this case it's weakness, sickliness, ugliness, and so on which constitute badness?

POLUS: Yes.

SOCRATES: Well, do you think there's also such a thing as psychological badness?

POLUS: Of course.

SOCRATES: Which consists, wouldn't you say, in injustice, ignorance, cowardice and so on?*

POLUS: Yes.

SOCRATES: So it's your opinion that there's a pernicious state for each of the three—for property, body, and c mind*—and that these are respectively poverty, sickliness, and immorality. Yes?

POLUS: Yes.

SOCRATES: Well, which of these three kinds of iniquity is the most contemptible? Isn't it immorality and psychological iniquity in general?

POLUS: Yes, that's by far the most contemptible.

SOCRATES: And if it's the most contemptible, it's the worst too, isn't it?

POLUS: Why should you think that, Socrates?

SOCRATES: Because it follows from our earlier conclusions that in any situation it's the thing which causes the maximum amount of unpleasantness or harm or both that is the most contemptible.

POLUS: That's very true.

SOCRATES: And didn't we just agree that immorality— that is, psychological iniquity in general—is particularly contemptible?

POLUS: Yes, we did.   d

SOCRATES: Either it's exceptionally unpleasant, then, and it's particularly contemptible because it exceeds the others in its unpleasantness, or it's particularly contemptible because it exceeds the others in harmfulness or in both qualities at once. Yes?

POLUS: Of course.

SOCRATES: Well, are injustice, lack of self-discipline, cowardice, and ignorance more unpleasant than hunger and exhaustion?

POLUS: I don't think we've found any reason to say that, Socrates.

SOCRATES: Why, then, is psychological iniquity more contemptible than anything else? If, as you say, it isn't because it causes more distress than other kinds of badness, it must be because it exceeds the alterna-
e   tives in harmfulness. In some sense, then, it causes an incredible amount of harm and is unbelievably bad.

POLUS: I suppose so.

SOCRATES: Well, if something causes more harm than anything else, isn't it the worst thing in the world?

POLUS: Yes.

SOCRATES: Doesn't it follow that psychological iniquity— injustice, self-indulgence, and so on—is the worst thing in the world?

POLUS: It does seem to.

SOCRATES: Now, which is the branch of expertise that rescues people from poverty? Isn't it commercial business?

POLUS: Yes.

SOCRATES: And which one relieves us of illness? Isn't it medicine?

478a POLUS: Of course.

SOCRATES: And which one saves us from iniquity and injustice? Is that too hard a question for you? Look at it this way. When people have a physical ailment, where do we take them? Who do we take them to?

POLUS: Doctors, Socrates.

SOCRATES: And where do we take people who do wrong and lack self-discipline?

POLUS: To appear before judges. Is that what you're getting at?

SOCRATES: And don't we take them there so that they can pay a fair penalty for their crimes?

POLUS: Yes.

SOCRATES: Now, it takes justice to punish and discipline someone correctly, doesn't it?

POLUS: Obviously.

SOCRATES: So commerce relieves us of poverty, medicine relieves us of illness, and the administration of justice b relieves us of self-indulgence and injustice.*

POLUS: That seems to make sense.

SOCRATES: Well, which of them is the most admirable?

POLUS: Which of what?

SOCRATES: Of commerce, medicine, and the administration of justice.

POLUS: The administration of justice, Socrates, by a long way.

SOCRATES: In that case, it must confer either more pleasure than the others, or more benefit, or both. Otherwise it wouldn't be the most admirable of these three areas of expertise. Do you agree?

POLUS: Yes.

SOCRATES: Well, is medical treatment pleasant? Do patients enjoy themselves?

POLUS: I don't think so.

SOCRATES: But it is beneficial, isn't it?

POLUS: Yes.

SOCRATES: The point is that medical treatment saves us c from a terrible state, and so it is worth our while to put up with the pain and get well.

POLUS: Of course.

SOCRATES: Now, which is the happier state to be in, as far as one's body is concerned—to receive medical treatment, or actually to avoid being ill in the first place?

POLUS: To avoid being ill, obviously.

SOCRATES: Yes, it does seem to be true that happiness consists not in losing any badness you have, but in not having it in the first place.

POLUS: Exactly.

d SOCRATES: Now, imagine two people both of whom are physically or psychologically in a bad state. One of them is receiving treatment and is being freed from his badness, while the other isn't, and so still has it. Which of these two people is worse off?

POLUS: I should say it's the one who isn't being treated.

SOCRATES: Well, we found that paying the penalty for one's crimes saves one from the worst kind of badness—iniquity.

POLUS: We did.

SOCRATES: The reason being, I suppose, that the administration of justice makes people self-controlled, increases their morality, and cures them of iniquity.

POLUS: Yes.

SOCRATES: Since psychological badness is the worst kind there is, it follows that the height of happiness is not to have it at all . . .

e POLUS: Obviously.

SOCRATES: . . . and the next best thing is to be saved from it, I suppose.

POLUS: That makes sense.

SOCRATES: Which we found to be a result of censure, criticism, and punishment.

POLUS: Yes.

SOCRATES: The worst state of all, then, is to have it and not to be saved from it.

POLUS: I suppose so.

SOCRATES: And isn't this precisely the state of an archcriminal, with his utter immorality, who successfully avoids being criticized and disciplined and punished
479a —in other words, exactly what, according to you, Archelaus and his fellow dictators, rhetoricians, and political leaders have managed to do?

POLUS: I suppose so.

SOCRATES: Their achievement, then, Polus, is not so very different from that of someone in the grip of an extremely severe illness who successfully avoids having the doctors exact the penalty for his body's crimes— that is, who avoids medical treatment—because he's

58

childishly frightened of the pain of cautery and surgery. Don't you agree?   b

POLUS: Yes, I do.

SOCRATES: And he's afraid, I suppose, because he doesn't understand health and doesn't know what a good physical state is like.* I mean, the position we've reached in our discussion makes it seem likely that this is what people who evade punishment are up to as well, Polus. They can see that punishment is painful, but they have a blind spot about how beneficial it is, and they fail to appreciate that life with an unhealthy mind—a mind which is unsound, immoral, and unjust—is infinitely more wretched than life with c an unhealthy body. This also explains why they go to such lengths to avoid being punished—that is, to avoid being saved from the worst kind of badness. Instead they equip themselves with money and friends, and make sure that they're as persuasive as they can be at speaking. Now, if this position of ours is right, Polus, are you aware of the consequences, or shall we summarize them?

POLUS: Summarize them by all means, if you feel like it.

SOCRATES: Well, one consequence is that there's nothing worse than injustice and wrongdoing.

POLUS: So it seems.   d

SOCRATES: Didn't we also find that punishment saves one from this bad state?

POLUS: I suppose so.

SOCRATES: Whereas to escape punishment is to perpetuate the bad state?

POLUS: Yes.

SOCRATES: It follows that wrongdoing is the second worst thing that can happen; the worst thing in the world, the supreme curse, is to do wrong and not pay the penalty for it.

POLUS: I suppose so.

SOCRATES: Well, wasn't that the point at issue between us, Polus? You were calling Archelaus happy for getting away with terrible crimes without being punished e   for them, whereas I was upholding the contrary view. I was claiming that Archelaus or anyone else who does wrong without paying the penalty is likely to be far worse off than others; that doing wrong always makes people more miserable than suffering wrong does; and that evading punishment always makes people more miserable than paying the penalty does. Wasn't that what I was saying?

POLUS: Yes.

SOCRATES: And have I been proved right?

POLUS: Apparently.

Socrates concludes his bout with Polus by reintroducing rhetoric and arguing—not without irony—that it should not be used to evade punishment for one's crimes, but on the contrary for getting one's family and friends punished when they have done wrong, and for getting one's enemies acquitted for any crimes they have committed, because that is worse for them than being punished.

480a SOCRATES: All right, then. If what we've been saying is true, Polus, what particular use is rhetoric? What I'm getting at is this. We've reached a point in the discussion where we're bound to say that our chief concern should be to avoid doing wrong, because of all the bad consequences it'll bring for us. Do you agree?

POLUS: Yes.

SOCRATES: What if a person does do wrong, however, or if someone he cares for does? He should go of his own free will to where he'll find the swiftest possible punishment. That is, he should appear before a judge, as he would before a doctor, and he should hurry to

b   make sure that the ailment which is immorality does not become entrenched, rot his mind, and make it incurable. I don't see what else we can say, Polus, as long as our earlier conclusions remain unshaken. If we want what we're saying now to be consistent with what we were saying before, we can't put it any other way, can we?

POLUS: No, of course we can't, Socrates.

SOCRATES: So this rules out using rhetoric to defend wrongs, Polus, whether they're being committed by ourselves, our parents, friends, children, or country. We could only find a use for rhetoric, in fact, on the opposite assumption—that our first priority should c be to *denounce* ourselves and then, secondly, any of our family and friends who happen to be doing wrong at any time, and that we should make any crime they commit public rather than concealing it, so that they can pay the penalty for it and get well again. From this point of view we should require ourselves and everyone else not to flinch, but to put a brave face on it and submit courageously and fearlessly to the cautery and surgery of the doctor, as it were. With our sights set on goodness and morality, we should take no account of the pain. We should submit to the lash, if that's what the crime warrants, or to impris- d onment, if that's what we deserve. If we're fined, we should pay up; if we've earned exile, we must go; if the penalty is death, we should let ourselves be executed. We should be the first to denounce ourselves and the people close to us, and the use to which we should put rhetoric is to expose their crimes and save them from the worst of all conditions, immorality. Shall we commit ourselves to this view, Polus, or not?

POLUS: It sounds extraordinary to me, Socrates, but I e suppose to your mind it fits in with what we were saying earlier.

SOCRATES: The only choice we've got, then, is between undermining those earlier conclusions or accepting this view as their logical consequence. Yes?

POLUS: Yes, that's right.

SOCRATES: Now, taking the converse situation, and assuming that in fact one should harm anyone (an enemy, for instance),* then as long as you aren't having wrong done to you by a given enemy—which is something to watch out for—and he's doing wrong to someone else instead, you have to use all your

481a verbal and practical resources to try to ensure that he does not get punished and does not appear before a judge! And if an enemy of yours does appear there, you have to come up with a way for him to escape and so avoid punishment! If he's stolen a pile of money, you have to make sure he doesn't give it back, but keeps it and spends it in godless immorality on himself and his acquaintances. If death is the penalty for his crime, you have to keep him alive, preferably for ever, so that he never dies and his iniquity goes on and on; but if you can't manage that, you'd better ensure that he lives in his state of

b wickedness for as long as possible.

These are the kinds of circumstances in which I think rhetoric has some use,* Polus. I can't see that it's any particular use to a person with no criminal intentions. Maybe it's no use at all in that situation: nothing came up in the previous discussion to make us think it is.

In exasperation, Callicles joins the fray. He cannot believe that Socrates seriously holds these revolutionary views. Socrates replies, in metaphorical language, that he is certainly voicing his inner convictions—and contrasts this with the worldly Callicles' obligation to voice only what accords with the changing whims of the populace. Callicles locates Polus' mistake as conceding that doing wrong is more disgraceful than suffering it. He claims that this view is merely a convention designed by the weak to suppress the strong and argues that might is right, by natural law. Socrates' aberrant views, he claims, are due to overindulgence in intellectual pursuits rather than worldly experience. Callicles ends his long and famous speech with a prophetic warning that if Socrates ever finds himself in court, his impracticality will leave him incapable of defending himself.

CALLICLES: Tell me, Chaerephon, is Socrates serious or is he having us on?

CHAEREPHON: I think he's perfectly serious, but there's nothing like asking the man himself.

CALLICLES: All right, I'd certainly love to do that. Socrates, may I ask you a question? Are we to take it c that you're serious in all this, or are you having us on? You see, if you're serious, and if what you're saying really is the truth, surely human life would be turned upside down, wouldn't it? Everything we do is the opposite of what you imply we should be doing.

SOCRATES: Callicles, if there weren't areas of overlap within all the individual variety of human experience—if a person's experiences were private and couldn't be shared by others—it wouldn't be easy to communicate one's own experience to anyone else. d I say this because I have an idea that you and I do in fact share an experience—that of having two loves each. I love Alcibiades the son of Cleinias, and philosophy, and your two loves are the Athenian populace and Demus the son of Pyrilampes.* Now, you're terribly clever, of course, but all the same I've had occasion to notice that you're incapable of objecting to anything your loved ones say or believe. You chop and change rather than contradict them. If e in the Assembly the Athenian people refuse to accept an idea of yours, you change tack and say what they want to hear, and your behaviour is pretty much the same with that good-looking lad of Pyrilampes'. For instance, you're so incapable of challenging your loved ones' decisions and assertions that if anyone were to express surprise at the extraordinary things they cause you to say once in a while, you'd probably respond— if you were in a truthful mood—by admitting that it's only when someone stops *them* voicing these 482a opinions that you'll stop echoing them.

And that's more or less what you're bound to hear from me as well, you know. So rather than expressing surprise at the things I've been saying, you should stop my darling philosophy voicing these opinions. You see, my friend, she's constantly repeating the views you've just heard from me, and she's far less fickle than my other love. I mean, Alcibiades says different things at different times, but philosophy's views never change, and what you're finding puzzling b at the moment is typical of what she says. You were here throughout the discussion, however, so it's up to you either to prove her wrong by showing, as I said a short while ago, that wrongdoing—particularly unpunished wrongdoing—is *not* absolutely the worst thing that can happen, or to leave this notion unrefuted. But if you leave it unrefuted, then I swear to you by the divine dog of the Egyptians* that it'll cause friction between you and Callicles, Callicles: there'll be discord within you your whole life. And yet, my friend, in my opinion it's preferable for me to be a musician with an out-of-tune lyre or a choir-leader with a cacophonous choir, and it's preferable c for almost everyone in the world to find my beliefs misguided and wrong, rather than for just one person—me—to contradict and clash with myself.

CALLICLES: Spoken like a true popular orator, I'd say, Socrates! All that passion! But it's only because what's happened to Polus is exactly what happened to Gorgias—and Polus told Gorgias off for letting you manipulate him into that situation. You asked Gorgias whether he'd teach morality to a hypothetical pupil of his who had come to learn rhetoric and didn't d already know what was right and what was wrong; and Gorgias, according to Polus, was embarrassed into saying that he would, because people would typically be offended if *anyone* said that he couldn't teach it. It was as a result of this concession that he was forced to contradict himself, and Polus went on to point out that this is exactly the situation you relish.* He was mocking you then, and I think he was right to do so, but now it's his turn: exactly the same thing has happened to him!

To be specific, where I think Polus was at fault was in agreeing with you that doing wrong is more

contemptible than suffering wrong. It was this admission of his which enabled you to tie him up in e
logical knots and muzzle him; he was just too embarrassed to voice his convictions. You pretend that truth
is your goal, Socrates, but in actual fact you steer
discussions towards this kind of ethical idea—ideas
which are unsophisticated enough to have popular
appeal, and which depend entirely on convention,
not on nature.* They're invariably opposed to each
other, you know—nature and convention, I mean—
and consequently if someone is too embarrassed to
go right ahead and voice his convictions, he's bound 483a
to contradict himself. This in fact is the source of the
clever, but unfair, argumentative trick you've devised:
if a person is talking from a conventional standpoint,
you slip in a question which presupposes a natural
point of view, and if he's talking about nature, you
substitute convention. On this matter of doing and
suffering wrong, for instance—to take the case at
hand—Polus was talking about what was more
contemptible from a conventional standpoint, but you
adopted the standpoint of nature in following up
what he said, because in nature everything is more
contemptible if it is also worse (as suffering wrong
is), whereas convention ordains that doing wrong is
more contemptible. In fact, this thing—being wronged
—isn't within a real man's experience; it's something b
which happens to slaves, who'd be better off dead,
because they're incapable of defending themselves or
anyone else they care for against unjust treatment
and abuse.

In my opinion it's the weaklings who constitute
the majority of the human race* who make the rules.
In making these rules, they look after themselves and
their own interest, and that's also the criterion they
use when they dispense praise and criticism. They try c
to cow the stronger ones—which is to say, the ones
who are capable of increasing their share of things—
and to stop them getting an increased share, by say-

ing that to do so is wrong and contemptible and by defining injustice in precisely those terms, as the attempt to have more than others. In my opinion, it's because they're second-rate that they're happy for things to be distributed equally. Anyway, that's why convention states that the attempt to have a larger share than most people is immoral and contemptible; that's why people call it doing wrong. But I think we only have to look at nature to find evidence that it

d   is *right* for better to have a greater share than worse, more capable than less capable. The evidence for this is widespread. Other creatures show, as do human communities and nations, that right has been determined as follows: the superior person shall dominate the inferior person and have more than him. By what right, for instance, did Xerxes make war on Greece or his father on Scythia,* not to mention countless

e   further cases of the same kind of behaviour? These people act, surely, in conformity with the natural essence of right and, yes, I'd even go so far as to say that they act in conformity with natural *law*, even though they presumably contravene our man-made laws.

What do we do with the best and strongest among us? We capture them young, like lions, mould them, and turn them into slaves by chanting spells and incantations over them which insist that they have to

484a   be equal to others and that equality is admirable and right. But I'm sure that if a man is born in whom nature is strong enough, he'll shake off all these limitations, shatter them to pieces, and win his freedom; he'll trample all our regulations, charms, spells, and unnatural laws into the dust; this slave will rise up and reveal himself as our master; and then natural

b   right will blaze forth. I think Pindar is making the same point as me in the poem where he says,* 'Law, lord of all, both gods and men...' And law, he continues, 'instigates extreme violence with a high hand and calls it right. Heracles' deeds are proof of this, since without paying for them . . .' Something like that—I don't know the actual words, but he says that Heracles drove off Geryon's cattle without paying for them and without Geryon giving them to him, presumably because it was natural justice for him to do so, in the sense that all the belongings of worse, inferior people—not just their cattle—are the c property of a man who is better and superior.

These are the facts of the matter, and you'd appreciate the truth of what I've been saying if only you'd forget about philosophy at last and turn to more important things. The point is, Socrates, it's fine for a person to dabble in philosophy when he's the right age for it, but it ruins him if he devotes too much of his life to it.* Even a naturally gifted person who continues to study philosophy far into life is bound to end up without the experience to have gained the accomplishments he ought to have if he's to be a d gentleman with some standing in society. In actual fact, philosophers don't understand their community's legal system, or how to address either political or private meetings, or what kinds of things people enjoy and desire. In short, they're completely out of touch with human nature. When they do turn to practical activity, then, in either a private or a political capacity, they make ridiculous fools of themselves—just as, I imagine, politicians make fools of themselves e when they're faced with your lot's discussions and ideas. In other words, Euripides was right when he said, 'A person shines at, and expends his energy on, and devotes most of his waking hours to, the activity at which he happens to excel.'* He shuns and reviles anything he's no good at, and sings the praises of his 485a own speciality in a self-regarding way, because he thinks this will increase his own prestige.

It seems to me that the optimum course is to have a foot in both camps. A certain amount of philosophy helps one to become a cultured person, and it's fine to take it that far; there's nothing wrong with studying philosophy in one's teens. But it's a ridiculous thing for a person still to be studying philosophy even later in life, Socrates. I feel the same way about

b doing philosophy as I do about stammering and playfulness. I enjoy seeing a child stammer and play games when he's still young enough for this kind of behaviour to be expected from him; it's pleasantly unaffected, I think, and appropriate to the child's age. When I hear a young child coming out with fluent sentences, however, it seems harsh, grates on my ears, and strikes me as degrading somehow. On the other hand, the phenomenon of a grown man

c stammering or playing childish games seems ridiculous and immature, and you want to give him a good thrashing.

That's how I feel about people who do philosophy as well. I don't mind seeing a young lad take up philosophy: it seems perfectly appropriate. It shows an open mind, I think, whereas neglect of philosophy at this age signifies pettiness and condemns a man to a low estimation of his own worth and potential. On

d the other hand, when I see an older man who hasn't dropped philosophy, but is still practising it, Socrates, I think it is he who deserves a thrashing. You see, as I said a moment ago, under these circumstances even a naturally gifted person isn't going to develop into a real man, because he's avoiding the heart of his community and the thick of the agora, which are the places where, as Homer tells us, a man 'earns distinction'.* Instead he spends the rest of his life sunk out of sight, whispering in a corner with three or four young men, rather than giving open

e expression to important and significant ideas.

I'm quite fond of you, Socrates, and that's why I react to you in the same way, as it happens, that Euripides had Zethus (whose words I quoted a moment ago) react to Amphion. I'm moved to copy Zethus talking to his brother, and say:* 'Socrates, you're neglecting matters you shouldn't neglect. Look at the noble temperament with which nature has endowed you! Yet what you're famous for is behaving like a teenager. You couldn't deliver a proper speech to the councils which administer justice, or 486a make a plausible and persuasive appeal, or put passion into a proposal designed to help someone else.' And yet, my dear Socrates—now, please don't get cross: it's because I'm fond of you that I'm going to say this—isn't this state an embarrassment for you and anyone else who keeps going deeper and deeper into philosophy? The point is that if you or any of your sort were seized and taken away to prison, unjustly accused of some crime, you'd be incapable—as I'm sure you're well aware—of doing anything for yourself. With your head spinning and mouth gaping b open, you wouldn't know what to say. And if, when you appeared in court, you were faced with a corrupt and unprincipled prosecutor, you'd end up dead, if it was the death penalty he wanted. Oh, Socrates, 'What a clever discovery this is! It enables you to take a naturally gifted person and ruin him.'* It makes a person incapable of defending himself or of rescuing himself or anyone else from terrible danger; the best he can hope for is that his enemies will steal all his c property and let him live on in his community with no status whatsoever, which would make his situation such that anyone could smash him in the face (if you'll pardon the extravagant expression) and not be punished for it.

No, Socrates, 'please take my advice and stop' your cross-examinations; 'practise the culture' of worldly affairs instead, and take up the kind of occupation which 'will make your wisdom famous, and leave to others the subtle route' of spouting drivel or rubbish— these are the right kinds of terms for it—'which leaves you living in a deserted house'.* Don't model your behaviour on these quibblers, but on people who make a living and earn a great many benefits for themselves, not the least of which is prestige. d

*Socrates professes to be delighted to have found some-
one with the characteristics which will enable him to
test the truth of his beliefs. He first begins to undermine Callicles' Nietzschean individualism by arguing
that if it is better to obey the stronger party, then nature
decrees that it is better to obey the masses, since they
are naturally stronger than any individual. Callicles
protests, rightly, that by 'stronger' he does not mean
'more capable of enforcement', and under Socrates'
guidance says that the people he has in mind are the
cleverer (or more astute) ones. Some crude prodding
from Socrates makes him narrow this down further to
those who have applied their intelligence to political
matters and have the courage to ensure that their will
is carried out. These are the people who should dominate
others and have the lion's share of wealth and so on.*

SOCRATES: If my mind was made of gold, Callicles, don't
you think I'd be delighted to find one of those stones
which are used to test gold, especially if it was a
really good one? I could touch my mind to it* to see
whether it confirmed that my mind had been properly looked after, and then at last I'd know that I
was all right and that any further testing was super-
fluous.

e CALLICLES: What's the point of this question of yours,
Socrates?

SOCRATES: I'll tell you. I think in meeting you I've met
with just such a godsend.

CALLICLES: Why?

SOCRATES: If you confirm the beliefs I have in my mind,
then I can be sure these beliefs are true,* because it
occurs to me that for anyone to be able to test whether
487a   or not a person's life is as it should be, he has to
have three qualities. These are knowledge, affection,
and candour, and you have the complete set. I come
across a lot of people, you see, who can't test me
because they don't have your knowledge, and then
there's another lot who are knowledgeable enough,

but refuse to tell me the truth because they don't care for me as you do. Then there are our two visitors here, Gorgias and Polus, who have the knowledge and are fond of me, but are too easily embarrassed b to speak their minds. It's indisputable, surely, that they're riddled with inhibitions. In fact, their sense of propriety is so acute that they had the gall to contradict themselves in front of a large number of witnesses, and to do so on the most important matters in the world.

You're the only one with the complete set of qualities, however. You've had what many Athenians would call an adequate education, and you're fond of me. What makes me think so? I'll tell you. I'm c aware, Callicles, that the four of you—Teisander of Aphidnae, Andron the son of Androtion, Nausicydes of Cholarges, and yourself—tell one another your ideas, and I once overheard you discussing the question of how far intellectual studies should be taken. I know the conclusion you reached was that detailed knowledge was undesirable, and you advised one another to be alive to the danger of being subtly d corrupted by excessive knowledge. And now you're giving me the same advice you gave your closest friends! That's good enough evidence for me: I'm sure you really are fond of me. Finally, it's clear that you're not the kind of person to let any sense of propriety stand in the way of your speaking your mind; it's not just that you yourself have said you're not, but also that your earlier words confirm the truth of this claim.

So it's obvious how things now stand. Any idea of mine with which you agree during the course of our e discussion will by that token have been adequately tested by us and won't require the application of further tests, because it won't have been lack of knowledge or an over-developed sense of propriety that made you agree with it, and since you're fond of me (as you yourself admit), you won't have done so deceitfully either. In actual fact, then, our agreement about a point will be what conclusively demonstrates its truth.

What sort of person should one be? What should a person do with his life and how thoroughly should he devote himself to his chosen occupation? What should he be doing when he's young, and what should he be doing when he's older? The attempt to find answers to these questions is the finest work in the world, Callicles. You accused me of being misguided about these matters, but if I'm going wrong anywhere in my own life, the mistake isn't deliberate, I assure you; it's merely the result of stupidity on my part. So please don't stop the kind of criticism you began, but let me hear a convincing argument about what I ought to do with my life, and how to achieve that objective. And if at any time in the future you catch me acting in a way which conflicts with any point on which I agree with you today, you can regard me as a total dimwit and as so completely hopeless that you needn't criticize me ever again.

Would you go back to the beginning, though, and tell me again what you and Pindar mean by natural right? Am I right in remembering that according to you it's the forcible seizure of property belonging to inferior people by anyone who is superior, it's the dominance of the worse by the better, and it's the unequal distribution of goods, so that the élite have more than second-rate people?

CALLICLES: That's the view I expressed earlier, and you'd hear the same from me now.

SOCRATES: Do you distinguish between 'better' and 'superior'? I wasn't clear about this before either. Are you describing stronger people as superior and saying that weaker people should be subject to someone who's stronger? I think that was the point of your earlier claim that it's in keeping with natural right for big countries to attack small ones, because they're superior and stronger. If so, you're counting

72

'superior', 'stronger', and 'better' as synonyms. Or is it possible for a better person to be inferior and comparatively weak, and for a superior person to be relatively bad? Or do 'better', and 'superior' mean the same? Please can you define your terms more d precisely and tell me whether or not 'superior', 'better', and 'stronger' are synonyms?

CALLICLES: All right. I state unequivocally that they're synonymous.

SOCRATES: Well, isn't it natural for the general populace to be superior to a single individual? After all, as you yourself said a short while ago, it's the masses who make the laws under which an individual lives.

CALLICLES: Of course they're superior to a single person.

SOCRATES: Doesn't it follow that any regulation prescribed by the masses is being prescribed by the superior group?

CALLICLES: Yes.

SOCRATES: It's being prescribed by better people, then, e isn't it? You said that to be superior is to be better, didn't you?

CALLICLES: Yes.

SOCRATES: From the standpoint of nature, then, their regulations are good, since the people who prescribe them are the superior ones. Agreed?

CALLICLES: Yes.

SOCRATES: Well, to cite another of your recent statements, the general populace rules that equal distribution of good is right and that doing wrong is more contemptible than suffering wrong, doesn't it? Is that so or not? Be careful now: we wouldn't want it to be 489a your turn to fall prey to a sense of propriety at this point. Do they, or do they not, hold that equal rather than unequal distribution is right, and that doing wrong is more contemptible than suffering wrong? Come on, Callicles, please answer. Your agreement would count as confirmation of what I'm saying, because it would be the agreement of someone with insight.*

CALLICLES: Yes, all right, this is what the general populace rules.

SOCRATES: It isn't only convention, then, which states that doing wrong is more contemptible than suffering wrong, or that equality is right: nature endorses these views too.* So it looks as though you were wrong in what you were saying before, and also shouldn't have used the claim that convention and nature are opposites to cast aspersions at me and accuse me of arguing unfairly, in the sense that I know perfectly well that they're opposed, and so if a person is talking from the standpoint of nature, I steer the argument towards convention, and if he's talking from a conventional standpoint, I steer it towards nature.

CALLICLES: Won't he ever stop talking rubbish? Tell me, Socrates, doesn't it embarrass you to pick on people's mere words at your age* and to count it a godsend if someone uses the wrong expression by mistake? Of course I mean that superior people are better. Haven't I been telling you all along that 'better' and 'superior' are the same, in my opinion? What else do you think I've been saying? That law consists of the statements made by an assembly of slaves and assorted other forms of human debris who could be completely discounted if it weren't for the fact that they do have physical strength at their disposal?*

SOCRATES: Oh, I see, Callicles. How very clever of you. So that's what you mean?

CALLICLES: Yes.

SOCRATES: Actually, my friend, I've had a vague suspicion all along myself that this or something like it was what you meant by 'superior', and the reason I've been asking you all these questions is because I'm so keen to turn my vague ideas into a proper understanding of your meaning. Presumably you don't think that two people are better than one, or that your slaves are better than you, just because they're

74

stronger than you. Would you start all over again,
then, and tell me what you mean when you call people
'better', since you don't mean 'stronger'? And please
use a gentler form of instruction, my friend, otherwise I'll have to leave your school.

CALLICLES: You're not being altogether sincere, e
Socrates.

SOCRATES: Yes I am, Callicles. I swear to you by . . . by
Zethus, whom you invoked during your extended
assault on me, when it was you who were keeping
something back.* Anyway, please tell me now: who
are the better people, according to you?

CALLICLES: I mean the élite.

SOCRATES: But that doesn't explain anything. Can't you
see that it's you who are stuck at the level of mere
words? Tell me, what is it that makes people better
and superior? Is it greater cleverness, or what?

CALLICLES: Yes, that's it, definitely. It's greater cleverness, of course.

SOCRATES: Here's your position, then: a single clever 490a
person is almost bound to be superior to ten thousand fools; political power should be his and they
should be his subjects; and it is appropriate for
someone with political power to have more than his
subjects. Now, I'm not picking on the form of words
you used, but that, I take it, is the implication of
what you're saying—of a single individual being superior to ten thousand others.

CALLICLES: Yes, that's what I mean. In my opinion, that's
what natural right is—for an individual who is better
(that is, more clever) to rule over second-rate people
and to have more than them.

SOCRATES: Stop right there! Let's think about this asser- b
tion of yours. Imagine lots of us together in one
place (just as we are now!) with plenty of food and
drink available; and imagine that we're a miscellan-
eous bunch, in the sense that we cover the whole
range from strong to weak. Now, among us is a
doctor, let's suppose—in other words, someone who's

more clever than the rest of us about food and drink—
and it's perfectly plausible to suggest that he'd be
stronger than some of us and weaker than others.
Since he's cleverer than the rest of us, won't he be a
better, superior dietitian?

CALLICLES: I'd say so.

c SOCRATES: Is he to have more of this food than the rest
of us, then, because he's better than us? Wouldn't
it be more appropriate for him to use his position
of authority to distribute all the food, rather than
squandering it on himself? It's true that if he wasted
it on feeding his own body, he'd have the greater
share, but he'd also suffer for it. No, he should have
more than some and less than others, shouldn't he?
Unless he was actually the weakest of us, in which
case he should have the smallest share, shouldn't he,
Callicles, despite being the best? Isn't that so, my
friend?

CALLICLES: You babble on about food and drink and
d doctors and so on, but you're missing the point.

SOCRATES: Isn't your point that a cleverer person is a
better person? Well, is it or isn't it?

CALLICLES: It is.

SOCRATES: And that a better person ought to have more?

CALLICLES: Yes, but not more food and drink.

SOCRATES: I see. More coats, perhaps? The best weaver
should have a larger coat than anyone else, and should
go around dressed in more and more gorgeous coats
than anyone else. Yes?

CALLICLES: What on earth have coats got to do with it?

SOCRATES: When it comes to shoes, though, it stands to
reason that the larger share has to go to the best
e person—which is to say, the cleverest person in the
field. A shoe-maker presumably has to walk around
wearing larger shoes than anyone else, and more of
them too.

CALLICLES: What have shoes got to do with anything?
You keep coming out with this absurd nonsense.

SOCRATES: Well, if that kind of case is irrelevant,

perhaps you're thinking of someone like a farmer, for instance. He's a fine, clever farmer and good at his job, so I suppose he has to have more grain than anyone else and keep as much grain as possible for his own exclusive use.

CALLICLES: You're just repeating yourself, Socrates—saying the same things over and over again.

SOCRATES: Yes, and that's not all, Callicles: I keep saying the same things about the same issues as well.

CALLICLES: God, yes, I agree. You simply never stop going 491a on and on about cobblers and fullers and cooks and doctors, as if they had the slightest relevance to our discussion.

SOCRATES: Why don't you tell us what *is* relevant? What is it right for a better, cleverer person to have more of? In what respect is it fair for him to be up on others? Are you going to refuse to tell us, as well as rejecting my suggestions?

CALLICLES: But I can only repeat what I've been saying all along. The superior people I mean aren't shoemakers or cooks: above all, I'm thinking of people who've applied their cleverness to politics and thought b about how to run their community well. But cleverness is only part of it; they also have courage, which enables them to see their policies through to the finish without losing their nerve and giving up.

SOCRATES: My dear Callicles, there's a very obvious difference between the charges we're bringing against each other, isn't there? Your complaint about me is that, in your opinion, I'm constantly saying the same things, whereas I find the opposite fault in you—I think you never say the same things about the same issues. At one time you claimed that it was extra strength which determined which people were better c and superior, then later you said it was extra cleverness, and now you've come up with something else again: your present idea is that the superior and better ones are the ones with extra courage. Please, Callicles, let's get this over with: just tell us what is it that makes people better and superior, in your opinion, and what they're better and superior at.

CALLICLES: I've already said that they're clever at politics and they're brave. Political power within com-

d munities should be in the hands of people with these characteristics, and right consists in them, the rulers, having more than the others, who are their subjects.

Socrates raises the question whether Callicles' superior people are in control of themselves as well as of their communities. Callicles has rejected conventional morality, which commends self-control: he thinks that happiness involves self-indulgence. The superior man is precisely the one who has worked his way into a position where he can satisfy any and all of his desires. Socrates states the opposite view at some length and with considerable power, but Callicles continues to maintain his hedonistic position. Socrates therefore produces two arguments against the equation of pleasure and good.

SOCRATES: But what are they to themselves, Callicles?

CALLICLES: What on earth are you getting at?

SOCRATES: Are they rulers or subjects?

CALLICLES: What do you mean?

SOCRATES: I'm talking about each one of them ruling himself. Or is there no need for him to rule himself, but only others?*

CALLICLES: What do you mean, 'ruling himself'?

SOCRATES: Nothing complicated, just what people usually mean by it. That is, being self-disciplined and in control of oneself, and mastering the pleasures and

e desires which arise within oneself.*

CALLICLES: What a naïve thing to say! By 'self-discipline' you mean 'folly'.

SOCRATES: I can't believe you said that. I don't see how anyone could fail to appreciate that I mean no such thing.

CALLICLES: No, Socrates, that's *exactly* what you mean, because human happiness is incompatible with enslavement to anyone.* What nature approves and sanctions, on the other hand—I'm going to speak bluntly to you now—is this: the only authentic way of life is to do nothing to hinder or restrain the expansion of one's desires, until they can grow no larger,* at which point one should be capable of 492a putting courage and cleverness at their service and satisfying every passing whim. Now, I don't think most people can do this, and that's why they condemn those who can; they're ashamed, and they try to disguise their failings by claiming that self-indulgence is contemptible, which, as I explained earlier,* is an attempt to enslave those who are naturally better than them. And why do they praise self-discipline and justice? Because their own timidity makes them incapable of winning satisfaction for their pleasures. b

Imagine someone born to inherit a kingdom, or someone who lacks this initial advantage, but has been equipped by nature with the resources for gaining some position of power—for becoming a dictator, for example,* or a political leader. In all honesty, could anything be more shameful, could anything be worse for these kinds of people than self-discipline and justice? They would exchange the freedom to enjoy the good things of life without interference from anyone for the voluntary acceptance of a master—namely, the conventions, opinions, and strictures of the majority. Under this wonderful regime of justice c and self-discipline, how could they possibly be happy, when even if they did have political power they wouldn't be able to use it to their friends' advantage and their enemies' disadvantage? No, Socrates, if you want to hear the truth (and you do claim that truth is your goal), it is that if a person has the means to live a life of sensual, self-indulgent freedom, there's no better or happier state of existence; all the rest of it—the pretty words, the unnatural, man-made conventions—they're all just pointless trumpery.

SOCRATES: Thank you, Callicles, for this generous and d

frank elaboration of your position. You see, what you're doing here is giving a clear account of things which other people think, but are reluctant to voice out loud. Please, I beg you, do all you can to sustain the momentum, until there's really no chance of our mistaking the right way to live. I have a question for you. We shouldn't restrain our desires, you say, if we're going to fulfil our potential, but should let them grow as large as possible and then do whatever it takes to satisfy them; and this, you claim, is a good
e   state of existence. Is that right?

CALLICLES: Yes, that's my position.

SOCRATES: So the idea that people who need nothing are happy is wrong?

CALLICLES: Yes, because otherwise there'd be nothing happier than a stone or a corpse.

SOCRATES: But the people *you* are calling happy have a terrifying life as well. The point is, you see, that it wouldn't surprise me if Euripides' words were true: 'Who's to say whether life might not be death and death life?'* Perhaps we really are corpses! In fact, I
493a   did once also hear a wise man claim that we *are* dead and that the body is a tomb,* and that the part of the mind which contains the desires is in fact characterized by its susceptibility and its instability. It was this part of the mind, it seems, which a clever story-teller (from Sicily, perhaps, or Italy) called a 'jar', although he derived the name from the fact that it is plausible and persuasive;* he also identified fools with non-initiates and said about the part of the mind
b   where the desires are located that in fools (which is to say, when this part is in an unrestrained and uncapped state)* it is a leaky jar—this is his analogy for its insatiability. His position is the opposite of yours, Callicles: he produces evidence to suggest that there's no one in Hades (by which he means all that is unseen)* worse off than these non-initiates, who go about trying to fill one leaky jar with water they bring to it in another equally leaky vessel, a sieve.

According to my source, the story-teller's 'sieve' is the mind: he used the image of a sieve to imply that c the minds of fools are leaky, in the sense that they're too unreliable and forgetful to prevent things spilling out.

This is pretty extraordinary stuff, I suppose, but it does clarify the evidence which I'd like to use to persuade you, if I possibly can, to change your mind— to prefer an orderly life, in which one is perfectly content with whatever is to hand, to a self-indulgent life of insatiable desire. Am I getting through to you at all? Instead of your previous view, do you accept d that self-discipline makes for greater happiness than self-indulgence? Or will it make no difference at all to what you think even if I tell you story after story with the same moral?

CALLICLES: Now you're nearer the mark, Socrates.

SOCRATES: All right, here's another analogy from the same school as the one I've just reported. Would you accept something along the following lines as an image for the different ways our self-controlled person and our self-indulgent person live? Imagine that both of them have a number of jars. The jars belonging to one of them are intact and are filled variously with e wine, honey, milk, and so on and so forth. And suppose that each of these liquids is rare and hard to come by, and that it takes a great deal of strenuous work to get them. Now, once our first man has filled up his jars, he stops channelling the liquids into his jars and gives them no further thought; as far as they're concerned, he can rest easy. The other character, however, is just as capable of getting the liquids—albeit with the same degree of difficulty—but his vessels are cracked and flawed, and he's forced to work day and night at keeping them full, or else 494a suffer terribly. If this is what the two lives are like, then, would you say that a life of self-indulgence is happier than one of self-restraint? Does this argument of mine make any impression on you or not?

Do you begin to agree that that a life of restraint is better than a life of indulgence?

CALLICLES: No, I'm not convinced, Socrates, because the one with the full jars can no longer feel pleasure,* and that, as I said a moment ago, is the life of a stone—for a person to be fully satisfied and so to stop feeling either pleasure or distress. An enjoyable

b life, on the contrary, consists in keeping as much pouring in as possible.

SOCRATES: But if there's a lot of stuff pouring in, there has to be a lot of stuff leaving as well, doesn't there? So the jars must be very leaky to let it all out, mustn't they?

CALLICLES: Yes.

SOCRATES: Now you are talking about living like a gully-bird,* rather than a stone or a corpse. Tell me, though: is being hungry, and eating when one's hungry, an example of the kind of thing you're thinking of?

CALLICLES: Yes.

c SOCRATES: And being thirsty and drinking when one's thirsty?

CALLICLES: Yes, and experiencing desire in all its other forms too, and being able to feel pleasure as a result of satisfying it and so to live happily.

SOCRATES: Thank you very much. This is an excellent beginning, and I hope you can carry on in the same vein without embarrassment. Actually, I'd better suppress my sense of propriety too, it seems. The main question I want to ask is whether a lifetime spent scratching, itching and scratching, no end of scratching, is also a life of happiness.

d CALLICLES: It's incredible, Socrates, how your arguments are designed purely for popular appeal.

SOCRATES: Well, Callicles, that may explain my success in shocking Polus and Gorgias and making *them* feel embarrassed, but there's no way to shock or embarrass you—you're too brave for that. So please just answer my question.

CALLICLES: Well, I'd say that a life spent scratching is a pleasant life.

SOCRATES: And a happy life too, then, since it's pleasant?

CALLICLES: Yes.

SOCRATES: Is that the case only if his scratching is re- e stricted to his head or . . . ? Shall I continue this line of questioning? What would you say, Callicles, if you were faced with the whole sequence of related questions? At the head of the relevant list is the life of a male prostitute—isn't this a terrible, shocking, miserable life? I can't believe you'd go so far as to claim that the endless satisfaction of his needs will make him happy.

CALLICLES: Doesn't it embarrass you to steer the argument in this distasteful direction, Socrates?

SOCRATES: Is it me who steers it there, Callicles, or is this direction prompted by the reckless assertion that people are happy if they're feeling pleasure, no matter what the source of the pleasure—that is, by the failure to distinguish between good and bad pleas- 495a ures?* Could you tell me once and for all whether in your opinion the pleasant and the good are the same, or whether there's even one pleasure which isn't good?

CALLICLES: I can't say they're different and still be consistent, so I'll say they're the same.

SOCRATES: You're breaking your original promise,* Callicles. If what you say contradicts what you really think, your value as my partner in searching for the truth will be at an end.

CALLICLES: You don't always say what you think either, b Socrates.

SOCRATES: Well, if that's true, it only makes me just as wrong as you. But are you really sure, Callicles, that unrestricted pleasure is good? If it is, all those shocking consequences I hinted at a moment ago will obviously follow, and a lot more besides.

CALLICLES: So you say, Socrates.

SOCRATES: But you're committed to this view, are you, Callicles?

CALLICLES: Yes.

c SOCRATES: So we can set about our discussion on the assumption that you're serious?

CALLICLES: We certainly can.

SOCRATES: All right, then. Since that's how you feel, here's something for you to sort out. There's something you call knowledge, presumably?

CALLICLES: Yes.

SOCRATES: And weren't you talking a short while ago* about a situation in which both knowledge and courage were involved at once?

CALLICLES: Yes, I was.

SOCRATES: It's because you think of courage as being different from knowledge that you spoke of them as two separate qualities, surely?*

CALLICLES: Certainly.

SOCRATES: Now, do you think pleasure is the same as knowledge or different?

d CALLICLES: What an intelligent question! It's different, of course.

SOCRATES: And is courage different from pleasure as well?

CALLICLES: Of course.

SOCRATES: All right, let's have it on record that Callicles of Acharnae* claims that 'pleasant' and 'good' are identical, but that knowledge and courage are different from each other and from goodness.

CALLICLES: And what shall we say about Socrates of Alopece? Does he or does he not agree with Callicles?

e SOCRATES: He does not. What's more, I think that after proper reflection about his own state, Callicles will disagree too. Here's a question for you. Wouldn't you say that people who live well are in the opposite situation from those who live badly?

CALLICLES: Yes.

SOCRATES: Now, if these two states are opposed to each other, then the same principle which applies to health and illness is bound to apply to them as well, isn't it?

I mean, it isn't possible for a person to be healthy and ill at the same time, or to get rid of health and sickness at the same time.

CALLICLES: What do you mean?

SOCRATES: Well, any part of the body you want to take should illustrate my point, if you think about it. For instance, you know that a person's eyes can be in a 496a diseased state, and we say he's got an eye infection?

CALLICLES: Of course.

SOCRATES: He hasn't also got healthy eyes at the same time, has he?

CALLICLES: Of course not.

SOCRATES: What about when he gets rid of his eye infection? Is he also at that point getting rid of his eyes' health too? Does he end up losing both at once?

CALLICLES: Certainly not.

SOCRATES: Because that's too incredible and preposterous a thing to happen, isn't it?   b

CALLICLES: Exactly.

SOCRATES: What he does, surely, is gain and lose each of them alternately, doesn't he?

CALLICLES: Agreed.

SOCRATES: And doesn't the same principle apply to strength and weakness as well?

CALLICLES: Yes.

SOCRATES: And to speed and slowness?

CALLICLES: Yes.

SOCRATES: Here are some other opposites—things which are good and things which are bad, the state of happiness and the state of unhappiness. What about them? Does one alternately gain and lose each of these pairs?

CALLICLES: No doubt about it.

SOCRATES: Whenever we find a person losing and keep- c ing things at the same time, then, we'll know that we're not faced with the good and the bad. Do you agree with me about this? Please think carefully before answering.

CALLICLES: Yes, I agree without any reservation at all.

SOCRATES: Now let's return to a point that came up earlier. When you mentioned hunger, were you thinking of it as a pleasant or an unpleasant experience? I mean the actual hunger.

CALLICLES: I'd say it was unpleasant. When a hungry person eats, however, that's pleasant.

d SOCRATES: I agree. I see what you mean, but the actual hunger is unpleasant, isn't it?

CALLICLES: Yes.

SOCRATES: Thirst too?

CALLICLES: Definitely.

SOCRATES: Shall I go on with these questions, or do you agree that need and desire are unpleasant in all their manifestations?

CALLICLES: Yes, I do. Don't bother with the questions.

SOCRATES: All right. Now, your position is that a thirsty person finds drinking pleasant, isn't it?

CALLICLES: Yes.

SOCRATES: When you say 'thirsty' in this situation, you mean 'feeling distress', I imagine, don't you?

CALLICLES: Yes.

e SOCRATES: Whereas drinking, which is satisfying a need, is also a pleasure?

CALLICLES: Yes.

SOCRATES: Now, your position is that the pleasant component of this situation is due to the drinking, isn't it?

CALLICLES: Absolutely.

SOCRATES: It's pleasant for a thirsty person, anyway.

CALLICLES: Agreed.

SOCRATES: Which is to say, for someone who's feeling distress?

CALLICLES: Yes.

SOCRATES: Do you realize what the consequence is? When you say that a thirsty person is drinking, you're saying that someone who's feeling distress is feeling pleasure at the same time.* Don't we find that it's the same aspect of oneself (I don't think it makes any difference whether one thinks of this as the mind or the body)* that is being affected simultaneously by these two feelings? Am I right or not?

CALLICLES: You are.

SOCRATES: Well now, according to you it's impossible to live well and at the same time to live badly.

CALLICLES: Yes.

497a

SOCRATES: You've agreed with me, however, that pleasure and distress can coincide.

CALLICLES: Yes, I suppose they do.

SOCRATES: It follows that to feel pleasure is not the same as to live well, and that to feel distress is not the same as to live badly either. And therefore the pleasant and the good are different.

CALLICLES: I don't know what to make of these clever arguments of yours, Socrates.

SOCRATES: You do, Callicles; you're only pretending not to. Now, press on. There's further to go.

CALLICLES: Why do you persist in this nonsense?

SOCRATES: So that when you scold me you can tell how b clever you're being. Isn't it the case that one's thirst and the pleasure derived from drinking stop at the same time?

CALLICLES: I don't understand you.

GORGIAS: Don't do that, Callicles. Please answer him. We'd appreciate it too, because without your reply the discussion will be incomplete.

CALLICLES: But all these futile little questions are typical of the way Socrates tries to prove people wrong, Gorgias.

GORGIAS: Why should that matter to you? In any case, it's not up to you to assess their value like that, Callicles. Just let Socrates test your views any way he wants.

CALLICLES: Go on, then. If that's what Gorgias wants, c ask your lowly little questions.

SOCRATES: It's all right for you, Callicles, you happy man. You've been initiated into the higher mysteries before the lower ones.* I didn't think it was allowed. Anyway, could you resume from where we left off and tell me whether one's thirst and one's pleasure stop at the same time?

CALLICLES: Yes, they do.

SOCRATES: And don't hunger and other forms of desire stop at the same time as the pleasure stops too?

CALLICLES: That's right.

SOCRATES: So we lose feelings of distress and feelings of pleasure simultaneously, don't we?

d CALLICLES: Yes.

SOCRATES: You've agreed, however, that we don't lose things which are good and things which are bad simultaneously. Have you changed your mind about this?

CALLICLES: No, I haven't. Why?

SOCRATES: Because the upshot is that good things aren't the same as pleasant things, and bad things aren't the same as unpleasant things either. You see, we can lose one pair simultaneously, but not the other, and that means they're different. How could things which are good be the same as things which are pleasant, then? How could bad things and unpleasant things be the same? But I don't think this argument of mine has won your agreement, so here's an alternative approach you might prefer. What do you think about this? You describe people as good-looking if they

e have good looks, and by the same token isn't it the possession of good qualities that enables you to refer to certain people as 'good'?

CALLICLES: Yes.

SOCRATES: Now, do you call fools and cowards 'good'? No, I don't suppose you do, because not long ago you were reserving the term for brave, clever people. Aren't they the ones you call 'good'?

CALLICLES: Yes.

SOCRATES: Well, do foolish children enjoy themselves, in your experience?

CALLICLES: Yes.

SOCRATES: And what about foolish adults? Have you ever seen them enjoying themselves?

CALLICLES: I suppose so, but what difference does that make?

SOCRATES: Oh, no difference. Just answer the question.

CALLICLES: All right, yes, I've seen that.   498a

SOCRATES: And do intelligent people find things pleasing and distressing, in your experience?

CALLICLES: Yes.

SOCRATES: Do clever people or thoughtless people experience more pleasure and distress?

CALLICLES: I don't think there's much to tell between them.

SOCRATES: Well, that'll do for me. Now, have you ever come across cowards during a military campaign?

CALLICLES: Of course.

SOCRATES: And which lot struck you as being more pleased when the enemy forces were falling back, the cowards or the brave men?

CALLICLES: I think they were both pleased—the cowards marginally more so, perhaps.   b

SOCRATES: That doesn't matter. But cowards feel pleasure too, do they?

CALLICLES: Certainly.

SOCRATES: As do thoughtless people, apparently.

CALLICLES: Yes.

SOCRATES: And when the enemy was advancing, was it only the cowards who were upset, or were the brave ones too?

CALLICLES: Both lots were.

SOCRATES: To the same degree?

CALLICLES: The cowards suffered more intensely, I suppose.

SOCRATES: And when the enemy was falling back, they were more pleased?

CALLICLES: Maybe.

SOCRATES: So what you're saying is that although thoughtless people and clever people, and cowards and heroes, feel pleasure and distress to almost the same degree, cowards experience these feelings more intensely than heroes. Yes?   c

CALLICLES: Yes.

SOCRATES: But it's the clever ones and the heroes who are good, whereas the cowards and the fools are bad. Isn't that so?

CALLICLES: Yes.

SOCRATES: Doesn't it follow that there's little to tell between good people and bad people in terms of how much pleasure and distress they experience?

CALLICLES: Yes.

SOCRATES: Are good people and bad people almost equally good and bad, then—or is it even the case that bad people are more good, in fact?

d CALLICLES: I haven't the faintest idea what you mean.

SOCRATES: Haven't you? Didn't you agree that good people are good because they possess good qualities, and bad people are bad because they possess bad qualities? And aren't you also claiming that there's no difference between good and pleasure, or between bad and distress?

CALLICLES: Yes, I am.

SOCRATES: So any pleasant experience is by that token the possession of good (that is, pleasure), isn't it?

CALLICLES: Of course.

SOCRATES: Their possession of this good quality, then, makes people who are feeling pleasure good, doesn't it?*

CALLICLES: Yes.

SOCRATES: And unpleasant experiences are the possession of bad qualities, or feelings of distress. Yes?

CALLICLES: Yes.

e SOCRATES: And it's the possession of bad qualities which makes bad people bad, isn't it? Or have you changed your mind about this?

CALLICLES: No, I haven't.

SOCRATES: So anyone who feels pleasure is good, and anyone who feels distress is bad?

CALLICLES: That's right.

SOCRATES: And aren't people good and bad to a greater or lesser or roughly equal degree depending on whether they experience these feelings to a greater or lesser or roughly equal degree?

CALLICLES: Yes.

SOCRATES: And didn't you say that fools and cowards experience roughly the same intensity of pleasure and distress as clever people and heroes, or even that cowards feel more, in fact?

CALLICLES: Yes.

SOCRATES: Could you help me work out the consequences of our position? I mean, it's worth repeating and reconsidering valuable points 'two and even three times', as the proverb puts it. We're saying that 499a people with intelligence and courage are good, aren't we?

CALLICLES: Yes.

SOCRATES: And that fools and cowards are bad?

CALLICLES: Yes.

SOCRATES: Aren't we also claiming that people who feel pleasure are good?

CALLICLES: Yes.

SOCRATES: And that people suffering distress are bad?

CALLICLES: They're bound to be.

SOCRATES: And that while there's little to tell between good people and bad people in terms of how much pleasure and distress they experience, bad people might experience more?

CALLICLES: Yes.

SOCRATES: This means that there's little to tell between good people and bad people in terms of how good and bad they are, doesn't it? And that, if anything, bad people are better than good people? Apart from what we've already said, doesn't the idea that pleasure b and good are the same have these additional consequences? I don't see how we can avoid this conclusion, Callicles, do you?

Callicles shifts from commending mere quantity of pleasure to admitting that there are qualitative differences between pleasures. This allows Socrates to reintroduce the distinction between means and ends. He argues that better pleasures are those whose longer-term effects are good (which in turn confirms that pleasure is not the good, since the good is something pleasure can aim for). The good life then becomes a matter of foresight, not immediate feeling response, and therefore arguably requires expertise. Socrates reminds Callicles of his earlier distinction between empirical knacks (whose goal is pleasure) and true branches of expertise (whose goal is the good). He counts rhetoric as a knack and criticizes all the great figures of Athenian history as mere flatterers of the populace, before sketching an outline of what true rhetoric would aim to do for its audience. In short, the expertise required to enable someone to live the good life is not the rhetoric Gorgias practises and teaches.

CALLICLES: I've been listening to you for quite a while now, Socrates. I've been saying yes on cue, but what I've been thinking about is the adolescent delight you take in seizing on any concession someone makes to you, even if he means it as a joke. Do you really think that I or anyone else would deny that there are better and worse pleasures?*

SOCRATES: Oh no! You're behaving terribly, Callicles.
c   First you claim that such-and-such is the case, and then that it isn't the case. This is the way you'd treat a child, and it's so dishonest!* I set out on this discussion in the belief that you were my friend and so wouldn't deliberately deceive me; but as it turns out, I was wrong, and now I've got to make the best of my situation (as the old saying goes) and accept this offering of yours. It seems that what you're saying now is that there are better and worse pleasures. Is that right?

CALLICLES: Yes.

d SOCRATES: Well, beneficial pleasures are good and harmful ones are bad, aren't they?

CALLICLES: Yes.

SOCRATES: Aren't they beneficial if they have a good effect and harmful if they have a bad effect?

CALLICLES: Yes, I agree.

SOCRATES: Are you thinking, for example, of the physical pleasures of eating and drinking that we were talking about not long ago—of how some of them make the body healthy or strong or good in some other way? Would you call pleasures of this kind 'good', and those which produce the opposite results 'bad'?

CALLICLES: Yes, that's it.   e

SOCRATES: Does the same go for unpleasant experiences? Are some good and some bad?

CALLICLES: Of course.

SOCRATES: Good experiences are the ones we should be going for, shouldn't we, whether they're pleasant or unpleasant? They're what we should be concerned with, aren't they?

CALLICLES: Yes.

SOCRATES: And hadn't we better avoid bad ones?

CALLICLES: Obviously.

SOCRATES: Yes, because Polus and I decided, as you may remember,* that the good in some form or other should be the reason for doing anything. Do you agree? Do you think, as Polus and I do, that all activity aims at the good, and that the good should not be a means towards anything else, but should be the goal of every action? Are you going to support us 500a and make it three?

CALLICLES: Yes.

SOCRATES: It follows that the good in some form should be the goal of pleasant activities (as much as of any other kind of activity), rather than pleasure being the goal of good activities.

CALLICLES: That's right.

SOCRATES: Now, is just anyone competent to separate good pleasures from bad ones, or does it always take an expert?*

CALLICLES: It takes an expert.

SOCRATES: I think we'd better remind ourselves of another view I happened to express while talking to Polus and Gorgias. As you may remember,* I held
b   that there are some procedures which are restricted to pleasure—that's all they have to offer—and which fail to distinguish between better and worse, but I also held that there are other procedures which do know what's good and what's bad. I proposed cookery as a typical example of a procedure which is concerned with pleasure (and I called it a knack, rather than an area of expertise), and medicine as a typical example of an area of expertise which is concerned with what is good. Now, for God's sake, Callicles, and for the sake of our friendship, please don't think it's all right for you to play games with me and answer my questions any old how, without caring whether you contradict what you really think—and at the same time please don't treat what you
c   hear from me as if I were playing games with you. Are you somehow unaware that there's nothing which even a relatively unintelligent person would take more seriously than the issue we're discussing—the issue of how to live one's life? The life you're recommending to me involves the manly activities of addressing the assembled people, rhetorical training, and the kind of political involvement you and your sort are engaged in. But is that the right way to live, or is this philosophical life of mine better? And if so, what makes it better? So perhaps it would be best for us
d   to distinguish these two ways of life along the lines I tried out just now, and then, once we've agreed that they're different, we should try—if there really are two ways of life—to see how they differ and which of them is the one to follow. Anyway, you may not yet have understood my point.

CALLICLES: No, I haven't.

SOCRATES: All right, I'll try to explain myself better. You and I have already agreed that there's good and there's pleasure, and that the good and the pleasant are not

94

identical; we've also agreed that there are certain processes and procedures for obtaining each of these two—ways of pursuing respectively pleasure and the good. But before I go any further, I'd better find out whether or not you accept even this. Do you?   e

CALLICLES: Yes, I do.

SOCRATES: All right, then. I wonder whether you'll also go along with the idea I suggested to our friends here—that is, I wonder if you thought at the time that I was right. I told them that to my mind cookery was a knack rather than a branch of expertise as medicine is, and I went on to say that one of these processes—medicine, in fact—had considered both the 501a nature of the object it looks after and the reasons for its actions, and could therefore explain its results. Pleasure, however, is the sole point of the other one's attentions. There's absolutely no expertise involved in the way it pursues pleasure; it hasn't considered either the nature of pleasure or the reason why it occurs. It's a completely irrational process—it hasn't itemized things at all, so to speak. All it can do is remember a routine which has become ingrained by habituation and past experience, and that's also what it relies on to provide us with pleasant experiences. b

Do you think this is a satisfactory account? That's the main question, but then I also want to ask whether you think there are practices whose province is the mind rather than the body, and which are analogous in the sense that while some of them involve expertise and work out in advance what will be best for the mind, others don't care about that and (as was the case with cookery) have restricted their thinking to how the mind gets pleasure; not only have they not given any consideration to whether there might be . qualitative differences between pleasures, they're simply not interested in anything except gratifying the mind, whether that is to its advantage or dis- c advantage.

The point is, Callicles, that I do think these practices

exist, and I maintain that pandering like this to the pleasures of the body or the mind or whatever, without taking into consideration the question of better and worse, is flattery. What about you? Do you endorse this view of mine or disagree?

CALLICLES: Oh, I agree—as a favour to Gorgias, and so that the discussion isn't left incomplete.*

d SOCRATES: Now, can this only happen to one mind at a time, rather than to two or more?

CALLICLES: No, it can happen to two or more.

SOCRATES: So if there's a whole crowd of people, it's possible to gratify all their minds at once, without considering what's best for them. Is that right?

CALLICLES: I'd say so.

SOCRATES: Can you tell me which activities have this effect? Perhaps it would be better for me to ask you specific questions and for you to tell me whether or not you think the activity I've mentioned does have this effect. Is that all right with you? Let's start with

e playing the reed-pipe. Do you think it belongs to this category, Callicles? Is its sole purpose to give us pleasure, without worrying about anything else?

CALLICLES: I think so.

SOCRATES: And so on for all related activities, like playing the *kithara* in competitions?*

CALLICLES: Yes.

SOCRATES: And what about training choirs to sing dithyrambic poetry you've composed?* Don't you think it belongs here? I mean, do you think Cinesias the son of Meles is the slightest bit interested in having his words improve his audience, rather than in finding

502a a way to gratify a packed theatre?

CALLICLES: Well, it's clear—at least in the case of Cinesias —that he's only interested in giving pleasure, Socrates.

SOCRATES: What about his father Meles? Do you get the impression that when he's composing music for the *kithara*, his objective is to maximize his audience's moral welfare? Actually, it might be truer to say, in *his* case, that he doesn't even aim at maximizing their pleasure, since they find his singing offensive! But anyway, what do you think about *kithara* music and dithyrambic poetry in general? Don't you think they were invented to give pleasure?

CALLICLES: Yes, I do.

SOCRATES: What about that grand and awesome pur- b suit, the composition of tragedies? What is the object of its efforts? Do you think the point of its earnest endeavours is merely to please the audience, or does it also struggle to avoid expressing sentiments which for all their delightful charm are morally wrong, and to include in its speeches and songs sentiments which are actually harsh and beneficial, whether or not people enjoy hearing them? Which of these two purposes do you think tragedy is designed for?*

CALLICLES: Well, there can be no doubt about *that*, Socrates. It's more interested in pleasure and in gratify- c ing an audience.

SOCRATES: And isn't that more or less how we described flattery a short while ago, Callicles?

CALLICLES: Yes.

SOCRATES: Next, suppose poetry were stripped of its music, its rhythm, and its metre. We'd be left with words, wouldn't we?

CALLICLES: Of course.

SOCRATES: Words spoken, in fact, before a large crowd—before the assembled people?

CALLICLES: Agreed.

SOCRATES: Poetry is a kind of popular oratory, then.

CALLICLES: I suppose it is.   d

SOCRATES: And 'popular oratory' is just another way of saying 'rhetoric'. I mean, don't you think poets are the rhetoricians of the theatre?

CALLICLES: I do.

SOCRATES: So we're faced here with a kind of rhetoric which is addressed to the assembled population of men, women, and children all at once—slaves as well as free people—and it's a kind of rhetoric we find we can't approve of. I mean, we did describe it as flattery.

CALLICLES: That's right.

SOCRATES: All right. What are we to make of the kind
e   of rhetoric which is addressed to the Athenian Assembly and the assemblies of other states, which are
attended by free male citizens? Do you think that
when rhetoricians speak, they want what's best for
their audience? Do you think they intend their
speeches to have the effect of perfecting their fellow
citizens? Or do you think they're really no different
from poets—in other words, that their objective is
the gratification of their fellow citizens and that the
common good means less to them than their own
private concerns? Isn't there, to your mind, something patronizing about the way they restrict their
dealings with the members of these assemblies to
trying to gratify them, and don't take the slightest
interest in whether or not they're made better or
503a   worse people in the process?

CALLICLES: There's no simple answer to this question, as
there was to the other one. There *are* speakers who
are motivated by concern for their fellow citizens,
but there are also others who answer to your
description.

SOCRATES: That's all I need. If the activity is twofold
like that, then one of its two aspects is presumably
flattery and popular oratory of the contemptible sort,
while the other is the admirable procedure of trying
to perfect the minds of one's fellow citizens, and of
struggling to ensure that the speeches one delivers
have the highest moral content, whether or not it
makes people enjoy listening to them. But you've
b   never come across this latter kind of rhetoric. If you
can think of any rhetorician who fits this description,
why don't you tell me his name?

CALLICLES: I certainly can't think of any contemporary
rhetoricians, anyway.

SOCRATES: Well, can you name a single rhetorician from
the past who's supposed to have been instrumental,

from his very first public speech onwards, in changing
the Athenian people from the terrible state they'd
been in before to a better one? If you can, please do
so, because I don't know who it is.

CALLICLES: But what about Themistocles? People say he c
was a good man, don't they? And then there are
Cimon and Miltiades and Pericles, who's only recently died, and you actually heard him speak.*

SOCRATES: Yes, Callicles, they were good men all right
—that is, if your earlier description of goodness
was true and it consists in satisfying your own and
others' desires. But if that's not the case, if there's
some truth in the conclusions the subsequent discussion led us inexorably towards, and we should
satisfy only those desires whose fulfilment makes us
better people, not those whose fulfilment makes us d
worse—and we decided that this whole area was a
matter for expertise . . . well, can you say that any of
the men you mentioned were good in that sense?

CALLICLES: I don't know what to say.

SOCRATES: You'll come up with something, if you search
in the right way. Let's take an unhurried look, then,
and see whether any of them were good in that sense.
Now, speeches delivered by a good man—someone
who wants what's best for his audience—aren't aim-
less, but have a purpose, don't they? It's the same e
with all other craftsmen too: each of them bears in
mind his particular task and so doesn't select and
apply his materials aimlessly, but with the purpose
of getting the object he's making to acquire a certain
form. If you need examples, look at painters, builders, shipwrights—any craftsmen you like, in fact. Each
of them organizes the various components he works
with into a particular structure and makes them ac-
commodate and fit one another until he's formed the 504a
whole into an organized and ordered object. That's
what all craftsmen do, including the ones we were
talking about not long ago* who deal with the

human body—trainers and doctors, I mean. They order and organize the body, in a way. Are we in agreement on this or not?

CALLICLES: I dare say you're right.

SOCRATES: So it takes organization and order to make a house good, does it? And without these qualities any house is worthless?

CALLICLES: Yes.

SOCRATES: And the same goes for ships?

b CALLICLES: Yes.

SOCRATES: And for our bodies too, we're saying?

CALLICLES: Yes.

SOCRATES: What about the mind? Can a disorganized mind be a good mind, or does it take organization and order to make the mind good as well?

CALLICLES: We have to think so: the preceding argument leaves us no choice.*

SOCRATES: Now, what do we call the effect of organization and order on the body?

CALLICLES: I suppose you mean health and fitness.

c SOCRATES: Yes. Next, then, what do we call the effect of organization and order on the mind? What's the equivalent term to 'health' in this case? Can you come up with one?

CALLICLES: Why don't you tell us yourself, Socrates?

SOCRATES: All right, I will, if that's what you'd prefer. If you think I'm right, please tell me; but if you think I'm wrong, don't let me get away with it—show me why I'm wrong. In my opinion, we describe the processes which organize the body as 'healthy' because they cause health and whatever else constitutes a good physical state. Is that right or not?

CALLICLES: It is.

d SOCRATES: And we describe the processes which organize and order the mind as 'law' or 'convention' because they make the mind law-abiding and orderly —which is to say, they imbue the mind with justice and self-control. Agreed?

CALLICLES: I dare say you're right.

100

SOCRATES: So these are the qualities which that excellent rhetorical expert of ours* will be aiming for in all his dealings with people's minds, whether he's talking or acting, giving or taking.* He'll constantly be applying his intelligence to find ways for justice, self-control, and goodness in all its manifestations to enter his fellow citizens' minds, and for injustice, self- e indulgence, and badness in all its manifestations to leave. Do you agree or not?

CALLICLES: I agree.

SOCRATES: You see, Callicles, what's the point of giving someone whose body is ravaged by disease lots of wonderfully pleasant food or drink or whatever, if that's not going to increase his chances of getting better in the slightest, or on the contrary is even—as an impartial view suggests—going to decrease them? Am I right?

CALLICLES: I dare say you are.   505a

SOCRATES: Yes, I can't see that life is worth living if a person's body is in a terrible state. He's bound to have a terrible life, isn't he?

CALLICLES: Yes.

SOCRATES: Now isn't it normal medical practice to allow a healthy person to satisfy his desires—by eating or drinking as much as he wants when he's hungry or thirsty, for instance—but almost never to let a sick person have his fill of what he desires? Do you agree with me about this?

CALLICLES: Yes.

SOCRATES: The same goes for the mind, doesn't it, b Callicles? As long as it's in a bad state (which is to say ignorant, self-indulgent, immoral, and irreligious), we must prevent it from doing what it desires and have it keep strictly to a regimen which will make it better. Do you agree or not?

CALLICLES: I do.

SOCRATES: Because that's actually better for the mind, isn't it?

CALLICLES: Yes.

101

SOCRATES: Now, to prevent it from doing what it desires is to discipline it, wouldn't you say?

CALLICLES: Yes.

SOCRATES: So discipline is better for the mind than the indulgence you were recommending not long ago.

Faced with defeat, Callicles resorts once more to sullen abuse. Socrates continues the argument alone. The good life and human happiness depend crucially, he argues, on self-discipline. In fact, the whole universe can only function well as an orderly whole. The arguments he has been putting forward, and this cosmic perspective, provide the justification for the revolutionary view which provoked Callicles' entry into the discussion, that doing wrong is worse then suffering it.

c CALLICLES: I don't know what you're going on about, Socrates. You'd better find someone else to answer your questions.

SOCRATES: Our friend here can't stand people doing him good. In fact, he can't stand what we've been talking about—being disciplined.

CALLICLES: Actually, these arguments of yours don't interest me in the slightest, and I've only been answering your questions for Gorgias' sake.

SOCRATES: Well, what shall we do, then? Are we going to break off in mid-discussion?

CALLICLES: That's up to you.

SOCRATES: People say it's wrong to leave even stories
d unfinished, though: a story needs a head on it, they say, otherwise it goes around headless.* So please help our discussion get a head by answering the rest of my questions.

CALLICLES: You're a bully, Socrates. My advice to you would be to forget about the discussion, or at least find someone else to talk to.

SOCRATES: Any volunteers? No? Let's not leave the argument unfinished.

CALLICLES: Couldn't you complete the argument by

yourself? Couldn't you just talk to yourself and answer your own questions?

SOCRATES: Then I'd really have to be, as Epicharmus e puts it, 'capable of saying all alone what it took two men to say before'.* By the looks of it, though, I don't have any choice in the matter. All right, let's do it that way. Once knowledge of what is and isn't true in these matters is out in the open, we'll all benefit equally, so I think we should all try to be the first to get there. I'll tell you how I think the argument goes on, then, but it's up to you to challenge 506a me and show me where I'm going wrong, if any of you get the impression that I'm failing to recognize mistakes in my own thinking. The point is, you see, that I certainly don't speak as an expert with knowledge: I look into things with your help. And this means that if someone disputes something I've been saying and seems to me to be making a good point, I'm the first to admit it. But there's no point in me saying all this unless you think we ought to finish the argument; if you don't want to carry on, let's leave it there and go home.

GORGIAS: Well, I at any rate don't think we ought to go home yet, Socrates. I'd like you to complete the argu- b ment, and I get the impression everyone else wants you to as well. In fact, for my part, I'd like to hear you round the argument off by yourself.

SOCRATES: My own personal preference, though, Gorgias, would have been for our friend Callicles to have gone on talking to me, until I'd repaid him for Zethus' speech with Amphion's.* Anyway, even if you're not prepared to help me finish our discussion, Callicles, you must at least take me up on anything you hear from me which strikes you as incorrect. And if you do prove me wrong, I won't get cross with you as c you did with me. No, I'll make sure the public register lists you as my greatest benefactor.

CALLICLES: Just get the discussion over with, Socrates.

SOCRATES: Here goes, then. I'll review the whole

103

argument so far. Is the pleasant the same as the good?
No, they're different. Callicles and I agreed on that.

Should the good be the reason we do pleasant
things, or the pleasant be the reason we do good
things? The good should be the reason we do pleasant things.

d   Isn't it the quality of being pleasant which makes
us enjoy things, and the quality of being good which
makes us good? Yes.

Now, what does it take to be a good human being? What does it take to be a good anything, in
fact? It always takes a specific state of goodness,
doesn't it? I don't see how we can deny that, Callicles.

And whether we're talking about a good artefact,
a good body, a good mind for that matter, or a good
creature, what it takes for these states of goodness to
occur in an ideal form is not chaos, but organization
and perfection and the particular branch of expertise
whose province the object in question is. Right? I
agree.

e   In every case, then, a good state is an organized
and orderly state, isn't it? I'd say so.

So a thing has to be informed by a particular orderly
structure—the structure appropriate to it—to be good,
doesn't it? I think so.

Doesn't it follow that a mind possessed of its proper
structure is better than a disordered mind? It's bound
to be.

But a 'mind possessed of orderly structure' is an
orderly mind, isn't it? Naturally.

And an orderly mind is a self-disciplined mind?
507a   Absolutely.

From which it follows that a self-disciplined mind
is a good mind. Now, I can't see anything wrong
with this argument, Callicles, but if you can, please
tell me what it is.

CALLICLES: Just get on with it, Socrates.

SOCRATES: All right. If a self-disciplined mind is good,
then a mind in the opposite state is bad. In other

words, an undisciplined and self-indulgent mind is bad. Yes.

Now, a disciplined person must act in an appropriate manner towards both gods and his fellow human beings, because inappropriate behaviour indicates lack of self-discipline. Yes, that's bound to be b so.

Well, when 'appropriate' is used of the way we relate to our fellow human beings, it means 'just'; and when it's applied to the way we relate to the gods, it means 'religious'. And, of course, anyone who acts justly and religiously is a just and religious person.* True.

He's also bound to have courage, because a disciplined person doesn't choose inappropriate objects to seek out or avoid. No, he turns towards or away from events, people, pleasures, and irritations as and when he should, and steadily endures what he should endure. It follows, Callicles, that because a self- c disciplined person is just, brave, and religious, as we've explained, he's a paradigm of goodness.* Now, a good person is bound to do whatever he does well and successfully,* and success brings fulfilment and happiness, whereas a bad man does badly and is therefore unhappy. Unhappiness, then, is the lot of someone who's the opposite of self-disciplined—in other words, the kind of self-indulgent person you were championing.

That's my position, and I believe it to be true. If it really is true, it looks as though anyone who wants to be happy must seek out and practise self-discipline, d and beat as hasty a retreat as possible away from self-indulgence. The best course would be for him to see to it that he never has to be restrained, but if he or anyone close to him (whether that's an individual person or a whole community) does ever need it, then he must let justice and restraint be imposed, or else forfeit happiness.

I'll tell you what the ideal is that we should set

ourselves to live by, in my opinion. We should devote all our own and our community's energies towards ensuring the presence of justice and self-discipline, and so guaranteeing happiness. That's what should guide our actions. We shouldn't refuse to restrain our desires, because that condemns us to a life of endlessly trying to satisfy them. And this is the life of a predatory outlaw, in the sense that anyone who lives like that will never be on good terms with anyone else—any other human being, let alone a god—since he's incapable of co-operation, and co-operation is a prerequisite for friendship. In fact, Callicles, the experts' opinion is that co-operation, love, order, discipline, and justice bind heaven and earth, gods and men. That's why they call the universe an ordered whole, my friend, rather than a disorderly mess or an unruly shambles.* It seems to me that, for all your expertise in the field, you're overlooking this point. You've failed to notice how much power geometrical equality* has among gods and men, and this neglect of geometry has led you to believe that one should try to gain a disproportionate share of things.

There you are, then. Now, either we have to prove this argument wrong, by showing that happiness does not depend on a person having the attributes of justice and self-discipline, and unhappiness on immorality, or we have to accept that it's true and try to see what follows from it. All those earlier conclusions follow, Callicles—the ones you asked me if I was serious about, when I claimed that we should denounce any wrongs committed not only by ourselves, but even by our family and friends, and that this is what rhetoric should be used for.* Moreover, the point Polus conceded out of embarrassment (according to you) has turned out to be true—that doing wrong is more contemptible than suffering wrong, precisely because it's worse than suffering wrong. And it's also true that for someone to be a genuine rhetorician, he

106

does in fact have to be a moral person and to understand morality, and this in its turn was the point Polus said Gorgias conceded out of embarrassment.

Against this background, let's consider whether or not you were right to fault me* for my inability to defend myself or any of my family and friends or rescue them from terrible danger. You say that I'm as vulnerable as a person with no status at all to anybody's passing inclination to smash me in the face (to use your forceful expression), confiscate my d property, send me into exile, or even, if worse comes to worst, kill me. And according to you, there is nothing more contemptible than being at the mercy of people like this.

Well, I've already stated my view more than once, but there's no harm in repeating it. I deny that being wrongly smashed in the face or stabbed or robbed by a cutpurse is the most contemptible thing that can happen to a person, Callicles; I claim that it's more e contemptible, and worse as well, to hit and cut me and my property without just cause, and I also claim that to steal, enslave, burgle, and in short to do any kind of wrong against me and my property, is not only worse for the wrongdoer than it is for me, the target of his wrongdoing, but is also more contemptible.

As I say, these are the conclusions we reached before, in an earlier phase of the discussion, and they're securely tied down (if you'll pardon the rather extravagant expression) by arguments of iron and 509a adamant.* That's how it seems to me, in any case. And unless you untie these bonds—actually, it might call for someone younger and more forceful than you—anyone whose opinion differs from the one I'm proposing at the moment cannot fail to be wrong.* All I'm saying is what I always say: I myself don't know the facts of these matters, but I've never met anyone, including the people here today, who could disagree with what I'm saying and still avoid making himself ridiculous.

b   Anyway, I suggest that the facts are as I've said. If so—if the worst thing for a criminal is to commit crimes (except that, if you could have a worse than worst, it would be worse for him not to be punished for the wrong he does)—then what kind of defence would it really be ridiculous of a person to be incapable of providing for himself? It would have to be the inability to avert what does us the most harm, wouldn't it? It has to be a person's failure to provide that kind of defence for himself, his family, and his friends which is most contemptible, hasn't it? And then the second most contemptible failure is failure to defend oneself against what does us the second

c   most harm, the third most contemptible is failure in respect of what does us the third most harm, and so on and so forth, on the same principle that it's the amount of harm a thing does which determines how admirable the ability to defend oneself against it is and how contemptible the inability is. Am I right, Callicles, or not?

CALLICLES: You're right.

Obviously, the best course is to avoid both doing and suffering wrong. But how do we achieve this? It seems that in a political context one can only avoid suffering wrong by doing wrong. Practical politics, as it stands, ignores quality of life (which is what true expertise at living would produce) in favour of simply staying alive by pandering to the whims of the powers that be. Politicians consistently fail to exhibit the slightest expertise at improving people. In fact, there have never been any true statesmen in Athens; the only candidates turn out to be practitioners of flattery—and rhetoric is a type of flattery which is actually more contemptible than sophistry.

SOCRATES: So we're saying that of the two—doing wrong and suffering wrong—doing wrong is the greater evil and suffering wrong is the lesser evil. How can we manage to protect ourselves, then, in such a way that we gain both advantages—that of not doing wrong, d and that of not suffering wrong? Does it take ability or will? What I mean is, will someone avoid suffering wrong if he doesn't want to suffer wrong, or if he's equipped with the ability to avoid suffering wrong?

CALLICLES: Obviously the latter, the ability to avoid suffering wrong.

SOCRATES: And what about doing wrong? Is the wish not to do wrong all it takes for him not to do wrong, or for this to happen does he also need to be equipped with a certain ability and branch of expertise, which he e has to study and practise if he's to avoid doing wrong? No answer, Callicles? Well, here's another one for you. At an earlier stage of the discussion,* Polus and I felt we had no choice but to conclude that no one wants to do wrong, and that every wrong act is done unwillingly. Do you think we were right or wrong?

CALLICLES: I'll grant you this, Socrates, so that you can 510a get on and finish the argument.

SOCRATES: So it looks as though we need to be equipped with ability and expertise to avoid doing wrong as well.

CALLICLES: Yes.

SOCRATES: Well, what is the expertise that equips us with the means to avoid having any wrong done to us, or as little as possible? I wonder if you agree with my view, which is that either you have to actually be the ruler yourself (even the dictator) of the community where you live, or you have to be on good terms with the existing government.

CALLICLES: That's an excellent point, Socrates, in my opinion. Do you see how I'm perfectly prepared to b congratulate you on your good ideas?

SOCRATES: Well, here's another idea. I wonder whether you'll think it's a good one too. Friendly relations seem to me to exist particularly between people who conform to the wise old saw, 'Like to like.' Do you agree?

CALLICLES: Yes.

SOCRATES: So in a state which is ruled by a savage, barbaric dictator, the dictator is, of course, going to be afraid of anyone who's a far better person than him, and it'll be quite out of the question for him ever to

c   be wholeheartedly on good terms with him. Yes?

CALLICLES: Yes.

SOCRATES: And the same goes* for anyone who's considerably his inferior as well: a dictator would despise him and would never treat him with the respect due to a friend.

CALLICLES: Yes, that's true too.

SOCRATES: The only serious friendship a dictator can form, then, is with the same sort of person as himself—someone with the same likes and dislikes, but who doesn't mind being subject and subordinate to a ruler. This is the kind of person who'll be a big shot in a community with a dictator for a ruler; no

d   one will wrong *him* and get away with it. Isn't that right?

CALLICLES: Yes.

SOCRATES: So that's the course any young member of the community we're imagining must follow if he's wondering how to have a great deal of power and avoid being at the receiving end of wrongdoing. He must train himself from an early age to share the dictator's likes and dislikes, and he must find a way to resemble the dictator as closely as he can. Is that right?

CALLICLES: Yes.

SOCRATES: According to you and your lot, then, this is the kind of person who'll have gained the ability to

e   avoid having wrong done to him, and a great deal of power.

CALLICLES: That's right.

SOCRATES: Now, will he also have gained the ability to avoid *doing* wrong? Not at all, surely, because the ruler he'll have come to resemble, and under whose patronage he'll have gained all that power, is in fact unjust. I myself think the exact opposite will happen: as a result of this course of action he'll acquire the ability to commit countless crimes and to avoid paying the penalty for them. Am I right?

CALLICLES: I suppose so.

SOCRATES: In that case, it's the worst possible thing that 511a can happen to him: by impersonating this master of his, and by gaining power, his mind will be corrupted and warped.

CALLICLES: I don't know how you do it, Socrates, but you twist every single one of our arguments until it's back to front. Don't you realize that the impersonator we've been talking about will put your non-impersonator to death, if he wants to, and confiscate his property?

SOCRATES: Of course I do, Callicles. What do you think b I am, deaf? It isn't only you who've been telling me: I hear it time and again—from Polus a little earlier, and from almost everyone in Athens. But I've got something to tell you too. He may well kill him, if he wants, but it'll be a bad man killing a paragon of virtue.

CALLICLES: Yes, and isn't that exactly what makes it infuriating, on top of everything else?

SOCRATES: No, because one of the points of the argument has been that anyone who uses his intelligence will not find it infuriating. I mean, do you think it's important for a person to arrange matters so that he lives for as long as possible? Do you think the areas of expertise he should take up are the ones whose purpose is to keep us safe when danger strikes? Actually, one of them is rhetoric, and you *are* telling c me to take it up because it could offer me protection in the lawcourts.

CALLICLES: Yes, and it's really good advice.

SOCRATES: What about knowing how to swim, Callicles? Do you rate that highly?

CALLICLES: No, I certainly don't.

SOCRATES: But it *does* protect people against dying when

111

they find themselves by accident in a situation which calls for this knowledge. All right, you may consider this branch of knowledge trivial, but there are more important ones I can bring up, such as helmsmanship, which doesn't keep only souls safe in extremely dangerous circumstances, but bodies and belongings as well. It's equivalent to rhetoric, in fact. Now, helmsmanship is a modest, orderly branch of knowledge, which doesn't put on airs and gaudy attire and pretend to accomplish amazing feats. It achieves exactly what forensic rhetoric achieves, and so earns itself a couple of obols, I suppose, for bringing a passenger safely here from Aegina; or for the important service of bringing someone safely from Egypt or Pontus*—for keeping safe, as I was saying a moment ago, not only the passenger himself, but also his children and belongings and womenfolk—it earns, once it has put its passengers ashore at the harbour here, two drachmas at the most. And what about the helmsman himself, whose expertise has led to this successful outcome? He disembarks and goes for a stroll by the sea, near his ship, in unassuming attire. You see, he's intelligent enough to conclude that in preventing his passengers from drowning at sea, there's no telling which of them he's benefited and which of them he's harmed, because he knows that they were no better, either physically or mentally, when he put them ashore than when they embarked on his ship. He reasons as follows: if A, whose body is ravaged by incurable diseases, is in fact badly off because he didn't drown and die, and therefore hasn't been benefited by him, it's inconceivable that B's life is worth living, when it's his mind (which is more valuable than his body) which is riddled with incurable ailments, and there's no way it can do him good to be kept safe at sea or in a lawcourt or anywhere else at all. No, our helmsman knows that, once a person has gone bad, it's better for him not to live, since he's bound to live badly.

112

That's why, even though helmsmen save lives, they don't usually make a big deal out of it—and that's why mechanics don't either, my friend, although there are occasions when they're no less capable of saving lives than military commanders or anyone else, not to mention helmsmen, because from time to time they save whole cities.* You don't think of them as the equal of forensic orators, do you? And yet, Callicles, if a mechanic chose to make the kind of speech you lot make in praise of his line of business, he'd present an overwhelmingly strong argument in c favour of your becoming mechanics, on the grounds that it was the only worthwhile pursuit in the world. Nevertheless, you sneer at him and his branch of expertise, use 'mechanic' as a term of insult, and would refuse any intermarriage between his children and yours, despite the fact that the very reasons you give for approving of your own line of business make me wonder what justification you have for looking down on mechanics and the others I mentioned a moment ago. I know you'd say that you're a better d person and come from a better family, but if I'm wrong about what 'better' is, and goodness is in fact no more or less than keeping oneself and one's property safe, no matter what sort of person one happens to be, then it's ridiculous of you to disapprove of mechanics and doctors and all the other areas of expertise which have been invented for the purpose of keeping us safe.

No, my friend, you'd better consider the possibility that excellence and goodness do not consist merely in the preservation of life. Perhaps the mark of a real man is that he isn't worried about how long he lives, e and isn't attached to life. What a real man should do . is leave these matters in God's hands, believe his womenfolk when they tell him that no one can escape his fated end, and then consider how best to live however many years he still has to live. Ought he, for instance, to assimilate himself to the system of

113

513a government in which he finds himself? And to return to the present, should you therefore model yourself as thoroughly as you can on the Athenian people, if you're going to be on good terms with them and be a very powerful statesman? You should ask yourself whether you and I will profit from that, in the sense that we want to avoid what is reputed to happen to those Thessalian women who win the moon down from the sky. We'll win this political power of ours at the expense of what we hold most dear.*

If you're under the impression that anyone is going to hand you the kind of expertise which will enable

b you to be a political force here while you're *not* assimilated to our system of government (whether this means that you're better or worse than it), I think you've been misled, Callicles. If you're to achieve any kind of meaningful friendly relationship with the Athenian people—and you'd better believe that the same goes for Pyrilampes' Demus as well*—then it's not just a matter of impersonation: you have to be inherently similar to them. In other words, it's someone who can abolish differences between you and them who can turn you into a rhetorician and the kind of politician you aspire to be, because

c everyone enjoys hearing their own characteristic points of view in a speech and resents hearing anything unfamiliar—unless you tell me otherwise, my friend. Do you want to respond to what I've been saying, Callicles?

CALLICLES: I can't explain it, Socrates, but I do think you're making your points well. All the same, I'm feeling what people invariably feel with you: I'm not entirely convinced.

SOCRATES: It's the demotic love residing in your heart which is resisting me, Callicles. If we argued the issues through over and over again, you'd be won

d over. Anyway, I'd like to remind you of our agreement* that there are two procedures for looking after anything like the body or the mind, and that one

114

makes pleasure the point of the operation, whereas the other confronts its subject, rather than pandering to it, because it's concerned with what's best. Isn't that how we distinguished them earlier?

CALLICLES: Yes, it is.

SOCRATES: And of the two, the one which is concerned with pleasure is a despicable activity and is, in fact, nothing other than flattery. Yes?

CALLICLES: All right, I'll let you have that.   e

SOCRATES: Whereas there's nothing so despicable about the other procedure, is there? After all, our goal in this case is what's best for whatever it is we're looking after, body or mind.

CALLICLES: That's right.

SOCRATES: Well, surely, if we look after a community and its citizens, we should try to do so in a way which makes the citizens as good as possible, shouldn't we? Otherwise, as we discovered earlier,* there's no advantage in dispensing any other kind of favour: there's nothing to be gained by people being given a fortune in money or a position of authority or power 514a in any other form if their minds are imperfect. Shall we endorse this view?

CALLICLES: Yes, if you like.

SOCRATES: So suppose, Callicles, that you and I were about to embark on a career of public and political service and we were advising each other to undertake major construction projects, involving fortifications or dockyards or temples. The first thing for us to do would be to ask questions about ourselves, designed to try to find out whether or not we do have exper- b tise in the field of construction work, and who we were taught it by. Shouldn't that be the starting-point?

CALLICLES: Yes.

SOCRATES: And the second job would be to see if we'd ever completed any private building project for ourselves or for any of our friends, and whether or not it was an admirable piece of building work. Now, if

this investigation revealed that we'd been taught by
c   distinguished experts, and that we'd built a number
of admirable buildings (initially with their assistance,
but later on our own, once we'd finished with their
instruction), under these circumstances, it would
simply be a sign of good sense for us to embark on
a career of public service. But if we couldn't come up
with anyone who'd actually taught us, and if we'd
either built nothing or a lot of useless buildings, then
it would be sheer stupidity for us to undertake public
building work and to advise each other to do so. Am
d   I right or not?

CALLICLES: You are.

SOCRATES: And this is a universally applicable principle,
isn't it, whatever the field? Suppose, for instance,
that the advice we're offering each other assumes
that we're competent medically and the situation
is that we've undertaken to supply the state with a
medical service. I imagine that we'd assess each
other's competence. The kind of question you'd ask
about me is, 'All right, then, what's Socrates' own
state of bodily health?' Or you'd ask, 'Has Socrates
ever been instrumental in curing anyone else, from
any walk of life?' I'd ask the same kinds of questions
about you as well, of course. And if we found that
e   we hadn't been instrumental in making anyone of
either sex, from here or elsewhere, a better person in
terms of their physical health, then in all honesty,
Callicles, wouldn't it be truly ridiculous for us or
anyone to be so far gone in stupidity that before
we'd even treated a large number of cases (whether
successfully or not) and had gained an adequate
grounding in medical expertise as private practitioners,
we should try to learn pottery on the big jar, as the
saying goes, and not only undertake public medical
service ourselves, but also advise others who are in
the same position as ourselves to do so? Don't you
think it would be stupid to do that?

CALLICLES: Yes.

SOCRATES: The situation we're faced with, though, 515a
Callicles, is that you've just started public and political work yourself, and you're advising me to follow
suit and telling me off for not doing so.* What we
should do, then, is ask questions about each other
like, 'All right, has Callicles ever made any of his
fellow citizens a better person? Is there anyone—
from here or elsewhere, from any walk of life—who
was previously bad (that is, unjust, self-indulgent,
and thoughtless), but who has become, thanks to
Callicles, a paragon of virtue?' Tell me, Callicles, if
someone puts you to the test like this, what are you b
going to say? Whose name will you put forward as
someone who's become a better person as a result of
knowing you? . . . Why are you being so slow about
answering? Surely you accomplished something as a
private practitioner before turning to public service?

CALLICLES: You just love to win arguments, don't you,
Socrates?

SOCRATES: But that's not why I'm asking you these
questions. It's just that I have a genuine desire to
know how you think Athenian public and political
affairs should be managed. You've turned to politics,
and I think we should be told whether as a statesman
you're going to be interested in anything other than
how we, your fellow citizens, might improve. Haven't c
we already agreed time and again that this is what a
statesman should be doing? . . . Well, have we or
haven't we? . . . Please answer . . . Oh, all right, I'll
answer for you: we have. Anyway, now that I've
reminded you that this is the service a good man
should try to render to his community, please can
you tell us whether those men you brought up a
short while ago* were, in your opinion, good members of the community. I'm talking about Pericles,
Cimon, Miltiades, and Themistocles. d

CALLICLES: Yes, I think they were.

SOCRATES: Evidently, then, each of them, in so far as
he was good, left his fellow citizens better people

than they had been when he found them. Is that right?

CALLICLES: Yes.

SOCRATES: So when Pericles delivered his first speech to the Assembly, the Athenians were worse than when he was delivering his final speech. Yes?

CALLICLES: Presumably.

SOCRATES: There's no 'presumably' about it, Callicles. It necessarily follows from what we've already agreed— at any rate, it does if he was a good member of his community.

e CALLICLES: What of it?

SOCRATES: Nothing. But there's a question I'd like to put to you in this context. Do the Athenians say they were improved by Pericles? Don't they in fact make exactly the opposite claim, that they were ruined by him? That's what I hear people saying—that by instituting the system of paying Athenians for their services Pericles made them idle, work-shy, garrulous, and mercenary.*

CALLICLES: You've been listening to the mangled-ear brigade, Socrates.

SOCRATES: Well, here's something that isn't mere hearsay. You know as well as I that although Pericles was popular at first, and although at this stage, when the Athenians were still relatively bad people, they never convicted him on any disgraceful charges, never-
516a theless at the end of his life, after they'd become paragons of virtue under his influence, they convicted him of embezzlement and came pretty close to condemning him to death, which clearly indicates that they regarded him as steeped in vice.

CALLICLES: So what? Does that make Pericles a bad man?*

SOCRATES: Well, the analogous situation would make us think badly of a herdsman who was in charge of donkeys or horses or cattle—that is, if the creatures didn't kick or butt or bite him when he took them over, but eventually became vicious enough to do all these things. I mean, don't you regard anyone who takes over relatively tame creatures and then makes them fiercer than they were when he got them as a bad herdsman? Well, do you agree? b

CALLICLES: All right, I agree—as a favour to you.

SOCRATES: Well, do me the favour of answering my next question, then. Is a human being a living creature, or not?

CALLICLES: Of course he is.

SOCRATES: And Pericles was in charge of human beings, wasn't he?

CALLICLES: Yes.

SOCRATES: In that case, since he was in charge of them and he was a good statesman, what he should have done is leave them more moral than when he found them, shouldn't he? That's what we decided a mo- c ment ago.

CALLICLES: Yes.

SOCRATES: Now, to be moral is to be tame, isn't it? That's what Homer says.* What do *you* think?

CALLICLES: I agree.

SOCRATES: But Pericles left them wilder than he found them, and wilder towards him as well, which must have been the last thing he wanted.

CALLICLES: Would you like me to agree with you?

SOCRATES: Yes, if you think I'm right.

CALLICLES: All right, I dare say you're right.

SOCRATES: Now, if they were wilder, they were less moral and therefore worse people, weren't they?

CALLICLES: I dare say. d

SOCRATES: It follows from this argument, then, that Pericles was not a good statesman.

CALLICLES: So *you* say.

SOCRATES: So do you, actually; it follows from points to which you've agreed. But now let's turn to Cimon. Didn't these wards of his ostracize him, so as not to have to listen to a speech of his for ten years? And didn't they do exactly the same to Themistocles, and sentence him to exile as well?* As for Miltiades, the

119

hero of Marathon, they voted to throw him into the
e   pit, and if the chairman of the executive committee
hadn't intervened, the sentence would have been
carried out.* But none of this would have happened
to these people if they were good men, which is what
you're claiming. I mean, good wagoners—ones who
don't get thrown out of their wagons in the first
place—don't start getting thrown out *after* they've
been looking after their horses and have improved as
wagoners. This doesn't happen in wagoneering, and
it doesn't happen in any other job either. Do you
think it does?

CALLICLES: No, I don't.

SOCRATES: It looks as though I was right, then, when I
said earlier* that, as far as we can tell, there's never
517a   been a single good statesman here in Athens. You
agreed that none of the current lot fitted this description, but you thought some of our past statesmen
might, and you picked on the four we've been talking about. But now we've found that there's no difference between them and today's politicians. The
upshot is that, in so far as they were rhetoricians, the
kind of rhetoric they practised was neither authentic
nor successfully flattering, otherwise they wouldn't
have been thrown out.

CALLICLES: All the same, Socrates, none of today's lot
could even come close to matching the achievements
b   of any of the four we've been talking about.

SOCRATES: Callicles, I'm actually not criticizing them in
their capacity as servants of the state. In fact, I think
they were better at serving the state than current
politicians are, in the sense that they were more capable of fulfilling the state's needs. However, it's more
or less true to say that they were no better than current politicians as regards the only responsibility a
good member of a community has—that is, altering
the community's needs rather than going along with
them, and persuading, or even forcing, their fellow
c   citizens to adopt a course of action which would

result in their becoming better people. Still, I also agree with you that they were cleverer than current politicians at coming up with ships, fortifications, dockyards, and so on and so forth.*

Anyway, this discussion of ours is a strange business. We're spending the whole conversation going round in circles and constantly returning to the same point, without realizing the implications of what the other person is saying. I mean, time and again, surely, you've accepted and realized that there are two aspects to the procedures we're talking about, which are concerned respectively with the body and the d mind. One of these two aspects is servility, and it is this which enables one to keep bodies supplied with food if they're hungry, with drink if they're thirsty, with clothing and coverings and footwear if they're cold, and with whatever else they happen to desire. I'm deliberately using the same old examples, to help you see what I'm getting at.

These items may be supplied by a retailer or an importer, or by someone who makes one of them— a baker, for instance, a cook, a weaver, a shoe-maker, e a tanner. Not surprisingly, given their jobs, these manufacturers regard themselves and are regarded by others as looking after the body, but this view fails to appreciate that besides all these techniques there's also such a thing as expertise in exercise and medicine, which really does look after the body. They don't realize that this kind of expertise should properly be the dominant kind, and should be allowed a free hand with the products of all those other techniques, because it knows—and none of the others does— which food and drink promotes a good physical state and which doesn't. That's why the rest of them 518a are suited only for slavish, ancillary, and degrading* work, and should by rights be subordinate to training and medicine.

Now, sometimes I think you understand me when I suggest that precisely the same considerations apply to the mental domain as well, because you indicate your agreement as if you're grasping my point. But then a little later you come along and claim that there were in the past truly good members of this

b community of ours, and when I ask who you mean, you propose some candidates from the political sphere, and I can't help thinking that this is exactly the same as if we were talking about exercise and I asked you to name some people from the past or some of our contemporaries who are good at looking after the body, and you replied in all seriousness that Thearion the baker, Mithaecus the author of *The Sicilian Cookbook*, and Sarambus the retailer were wonderfully good at looking after people's bodies, because they dispense respectively bread, savouries,

c and wine.

Well, I imagine you'd be cross if I said, 'Listen, Callicles, you don't have the first idea about physical training. You're talking about servants, people who fulfil needs without the slightest good or proper understanding of them. They stuff and fatten our bodies, if they're given the opportunity, and ruin the original quality of our flesh as well—and we compliment them on their work! People are too naïve to hold those who treat them to the pleasures of the

d table responsible for their illnesses and for the loss of the original quality of their flesh. Instead they blame anyone who happens to be there offering them advice at the considerably later date when their earlier indulgence resurfaces with its cargo of disease—as it does, because it contravened every principle of health. So these are the ones they'll blame and criticize and even harm (if they can), while singing the praises of those others from before who are actually responsible for their troubles.'

e This is a good analogy for what you're doing at the moment, Callicles. You're singing the praises of the people who gave the Athenians lavish treats and indulged their desires. They're reputed to have made

122

their city great, but no one notices that these men from Athens' past made her bloated and rotten, by 519a stuffing her, with no sense of restraint or right, full of trumpery like harbours, dockyards, fortifications, and tribute payments. So when the retribution I spoke of comes, in the form of weakness, people will blame the advisers who happen to be there at the time, and will sing the praises of Themistocles and Cimon and Pericles, who should be held responsible for their troubles. In fact, you'd better watch out, because when they lose what they originally had as well as what they gained, they might lay into you, and my friend Alcibiades will probably be for it as well,* when at the most you'll only be partially responsible. b

Moreover, there's a stupid phenomenon I see happening these days, and I'm told that people did the same in the past too. I notice that when the city starts criminal proceedings against one of their statesmen, they take offence and complain that they're being treated terribly. 'We've been the city's benefactors in so many ways,' they say. 'That's what makes it wrong for her to bring us down.' But this is a load of nonsense. How can it possibly be *wrong* for any state official to be brought down by the very c state he's an officer of? It rather looks as though self-styled statesmen and self-styled sophists are in the same position. For all their cleverness in other respects, there's an anomaly in the sophists' affairs: they claim to be teachers of virtue, but they often accuse their pupils of wronging them, their benefactors, by withholding their gratitude in some form, and especially by not paying their fees. But can you think of any- d thing more absurd than this argument? It claims that people who have had injustice removed by their teacher, and have had it replaced with justice—who have become, then, good and moral people—are acting with injustice, which is something they don't have. Doesn't that strike you as implausible, Callicles my friend? And do you see how you've turned me

123

into a real popular orator by refusing to answer my questions?

CALLICLES: Can't you speak without someone answering your questions?

e SOCRATES: It looks as though I can. Anyway, your refusal to answer my questions is making me go on at considerable length at the moment. Please, Callicles, for God's sake and for the sake of our friendship, tell me what you think. Doesn't it strike you as absurd for A to claim that he's made B good, and yet to criticize B for being bad, despite the fact that he's good and was made so by A?

CALLICLES: Yes, that does seem absurd.

SOCRATES: Well, do you hear the professional teachers of goodness* using this argument?

520a CALLICLES: Yes, but why mention them? They're not worth it.

SOCRATES: Why mention people who claim to be city officials and to be concerned with improving the city as much as possible, and then periodically accuse it of being beyond redemption? How can you distinguish one lot from the other? There's no difference between a sophist and a rhetorician, my friend, or at any rate (as I suggested to Polus)* no substantial or significant difference. If you realized that, you

b wouldn't regard one of them, rhetoric, as absolutely wonderful, and yet despise the other. In actual fact, sophistry is a more admirable pursuit than rhetoric, just as the legislative process is more admirable than the administration of justice and exercise is more admirable than medicine. I even thought that popular orators and sophists were unique in the sense that they couldn't resort to criticizing the object of their educational attentions for treating them badly, because in the same breath they'd also be accusing themselves of having failed to help the people they claim to help. Isn't that right?

c CALLICLES: Yes.

SOCRATES: And, of course, it would also be reasonable

124

to expect that, if they're telling the truth, they're the only ones who are in a position to give their services away without immediate payment. Think of any other kind of beneficiary—for instance, a person who's been taught how to run fast by a trainer. He's the kind of person who might refuse to pay up, if the trainer gives him the opportunity and doesn't agree on a fee in advance and get payment to coincide more or less exactly with the time when he imparts the gift of speed. I mean, it isn't slowness which makes people d do wrong, surely, but injustice. Do you agree?

CALLICLES: Yes.

SOCRATES: So it is precisely the removal of injustice which gives the person responsible for the removal grounds for never worrying about being wronged in the future. In other words—and this is all assuming that it's possible to make others good—he's the only one who can safely give his services away, don't you think?

CALLICLES: I agree.

SOCRATES: I suppose this explains why it's not at all degrading for a person to sell the information he has to offer in *other* areas of expertise, like building.

CALLICLES: Yes, that's presumably the explanation.   e

SOCRATES: Whereas when it's a matter of how a person might perfect himself and run his household or his community in the best possible way, it's considered disgraceful to refuse information until one's paid, isn't it?

CALLICLES: Yes.

SOCRATES: The reason for this, clearly, is that it's the only service which makes the recipient desire to do good back. Consequently, we take it to be a sure sign that a person has rendered this service if he, the benefactor, becomes a beneficiary in return; if he doesn't, we don't think he has. Isn't that what happens?

CALLICLES: Yes.   521a

Since Socrates is probably the only person in Athens who is concerned with people's moral development, he

125

is the only true statesman (for all his notorious lack of involvement in politics). That is precisely why he will be misunderstood and condemned if he is taken to court. But this is unimportant; what is crucial is to avoid immorality. An immoral person may be able to escape punishment in this life, but he cannot in the afterlife, where he will be known for what he is, judged accordingly, and punished (that is, cured). The more power one has, the greater the chance of corruption. We must therefore set our own lives in order before even considering gaining power over others.

SOCRATES: Please tell me, then, which of these two ways of looking after the state you're suggesting I follow. Is it the one which is analogous to the practice of medicine and involves confronting the Athenian people and struggling to ensure their perfection? Or is it the one which is analogous to what servants do and makes pleasure the point of the operation? Tell me the truth, Callicles. It would be wrong of you not to continue to speak your mind as candidly as you did at first. So do the same now: don't hold back, but tell me what you think.

CALLICLES: Well, I'd say it's the one which is analogous to what servants do.

b SOCRATES: Thank you for not holding back. In other words, you're recommending me to practise flattery.

CALLICLES: Yes, if you'd rather cast aspersions,* Socrates. The point is, though, that if you don't do what I'm suggesting . . .

SOCRATES: Don't say it. You've already told me often enough that anyone who wants to have me executed will do so. Don't make me repeat my reply that it would be a bad man killing a good man. And don't go on about how he'll confiscate all my property, because otherwise I'll have to repeat myself and say: 'He may take it, but it'll do him no good. He was wrong to

c take it, so he'll only put it to wrong use, which is contemptible—or, in other words, bad for him.'

126

CALLICLES: Socrates, I get the impression that you believe you're immune to all this, as if you lived in another world and couldn't possibly end up in court, facing someone who might even be a particularly corrupt and nasty piece of work.

SOCRATES: I'd really have to be a fool, Callicles, to believe that here in Athens anyone is immune to anything. One thing I'm sure of, though, is that if I do get taken to court and run any of the risks you're talking about, it'll be a bad person who's taken me d there, since no good person could take an innocent man to court. And it's quite possible that I'd be put to death. Shall I tell you why I think so?

CALLICLES: Yes, please.

SOCRATES: There may be one or two others, but I think I'm the only genuine practitioner of politics in Athens today, the only example of a true statesman.* So because moral improvement rather than gratification and pleasure is always the reason for my saying anything, and because I refuse to take the subtle e route* you're recommending, I'll be tongue-tied in court. The argument I used before, when I was talking to Polus,* is relevant to the situation I'll be in. My trial will be equivalent to a doctor being prosecuted by a cook before a jury of young children. How do you think a doctor would defend himself if he were up before that kind of court? The prosecutor would argue, 'Children, the defendant has committed numerous crimes against your honoured selves. He has ruined the youngest among you* with his surgery and cautery and baffled them with compresses and nauseants; he gives them harsh potions and forces 522a them to go without food and drink. He's not like me: I'm constantly giving you all kinds of delicious treats.' In these dire straits, what do you think a doctor could find to say? What do you suppose would happen if he told the truth and said, 'All my actions, children, have been prompted by a concern for health.' Can you imagine the hue and cry our jurors would raise at that? It would be enormous, wouldn't it?

CALLICLES: I suppose so.

SOCRATES: Of course it would. And don't you think he'd
b   be completely stuck for words?

CALLICLES: Yes.

SOCRATES: Well, that's an analogy for what will certainly happen to me if I find myself up before a court. In the first place, the only kind of good turn and benefit people recognize is pleasure, but I won't be able to provide them with an account of the pleasures they owe to me; in fact, I have no desire to emulate either the givers or the receivers of these favours. Secondly, if someone accuses me of corrupting youngsters by baffling them, or of voicing (either in private or in public) harsh and critical views about their elders, I won't be able to tell the truth and say, 'All my words and actions are prompted by a sense of justice'—adding 'gentlemen of the jury', just like
c   you and your fellow rhetoricians—and there won't be any other defence available to me either. God knows what will happen to me as a consequence of this, but whatever it is, I suppose I'll have to put up with it.

CALLICLES: Socrates, do you think it's all right for a member of a community to be in the situation you've described? To be incapable of defending himself?

SOCRATES: Yes, because there's only one thing he needs, Callicles, as you've admitted often enough; he has all the protection he needs if he's never wronged a
d   fellow human being or a god in anything he's said or done. We've agreed several times that there's no better form of defence than that. Suppose it was proved through argument that I was incapable of providing myself or someone else with this form of defence—*that*'s what I'd find embarrassing, and it would be equally embarrassing to be shown up in this way in front of a large body of people or just a few people, or even if it happened during the course of a

one-to-one argument. It would certainly infuriate me to die as a result of not being able to provide myself with this defence, but you'd see me greet death without any worries if it happened because I didn't know how to flatter people with rhetoric. It's completely irrational, and a sign of sheer cowardice, to e fear the mere fact of death, but the same cannot be said for fear of injustice, since arriving in Hades with one's soul* riddled with wrongdoing is the ultimate evil. If you'd like to hear an explanation of why this is so, I don't mind telling you.

CALLICLES: Well, you've gone into everything else in exhaustive detail, so you might as well do the same for this too.

SOCRATES: Pay attention, then, as they say. It's an excel- 523a lent explanation. I expect you'll think that what I'm about to tell you is just a story, but to my mind it does explain things, since it is, as far as I'm concerned, the truth.*

As Homer records, when Zeus, Poseidon, and Pluto inherited their father's dominion, they divided it between themselves.* Now, during Cronus' reign human beings were subject to a law which the gods sanction even to this day and which is as follows: any human being who has lived a moral and god-fearing life shall on his death depart for the Isles of the Blessed b and shall dwell there, and live a trouble-free life of perfect happiness; however, anyone who has lived an immoral and godless life shall be imprisoned in the place of retribution and justice, which is called Tartarus.* In the time of Cronus, and in the relatively recent past during Zeus' reign as well, living judges dealt with living people and passed judgement upon them on the day of their impending death, which made the administration of justice poor. So Pluto and the supervisors of the Isles of the Blessed came and told Zeus that the wrong kinds of people were getting through to both places.

So Zeus said, 'I'll put an end to that. The reason c

129

the administration of justice is poor at the moment is that people are being assessed with their clothes on, in the sense that they come before the court during their lifetimes, and plenty of people with corrupt souls are dressed in attractive bodies, noble birth, and wealth; also, when it's their turn to be judged, a lot of witnesses come forward and testify to the exem-
d plary lives these people have led. All this impresses the judges. Besides, the judges themselves are wearing clothes as well: their souls are enclosed within eyes and ears and bodies in general. All this—their own clothing and that of the people they're assessing—constitutes a barrier. The first job', he went on, 'is to stop people knowing in advance when they're going to die, as they do at the moment. Prometheus has already been told to put an end to this, in fact.
e Second, they'd better be judged naked, stripped of all this clothing—in other words, they have to be judged after they've died. If the assessment is to be fair, the judge had better be naked as well—which is to say, dead—so that with an unhampered soul he can scrutinize the unhampered soul of a freshly dead individual who isn't surrounded by his friends and relatives, and has left all those trappings behind in the world. As a matter of fact, I realized what was going on before you did, and I made three of my sons judges—Minos and Rhadamanthys from Asia, and Aeacus
524a from Europe. After their death, they'll set up court in the meadow, at the junction where the two roads branch off towards the Isles of the Blessed and Tartarus respectively.* Rhadamanthys will judge those who have come from Asia, Aeacus those from Europe;* but I'll give Minos the privilege of making a final decision if the other two are ever at a loss. In this way, the decision about which road people are to take will be as fair as possible.'

That's the explanation I've heard, Callicles, and
b I'm convinced of its truth. What are its implications? The ones I can see are as follows. It seems to me that

death turns out to be nothing but the separation from each other of two things, the soul and the body. Now, once they have been separated, each of them remains in more or less the same state as it was when the person was alive. It isn't just the body which displays its innate features and the attributes it gained as a result of treatment it received and things which happened to it. For instance, big people (whether c their build was due to nature or nurture or both) make big corpses once they're dead, fat people make fat corpses, and so on; anyone who wore his hair long will have a long-haired corpse; if he was a felon, with his body scarred and marked by all the floggings and other injuries he received while he was alive, his body is going to show these marks after his death as well; any broken or deformed limbs a person had during his lifetime will be visible in exactly the same state after he's dead as well. In a word, all or most d of the physical attributes a person has during his lifetime also remain visible for a while after his death.

Well, Callicles, I think the same goes for the soul too. Once the soul has been stripped of the body, all its features become obvious—its innate features and also the attributes the person has lodged in his soul through his behaviour in particular situations. So when people come before their judge, as Asians do before Rhadamanthys, for instance, then Rhada- e manthys makes them stand there and examines their souls one by one. He doesn't know whose soul it is; in fact, he might well get hold of the soul of the king of Persia or some other king or potentate and notice that it's riddled with defects—scourged and covered in the scars which every dishonest and 525a unjust action has imprinted on it, utterly crippled by lies and arrogance and warped by a truth-free diet— and he'd also see that the promiscuity, sensuality, brutality, and self-indulgence of his behaviour has thoroughly distorted the harmony and beauty of his soul. When he sees a soul in this state, he immediately dispatches it in disgrace to prison, where it will undergo the appropriate treatment.

b   What is appropriate? As long as the person inflicting the punishment is justified in doing so, then every instance of punishment should either help its recipient by making him a better person or should act as an example for others, in the sense that the terrifying sight of the victim's sufferings helps them to improve.* Those who are *benefited* by being punished (whether the agents of punishment are divine or human) are those whose faults are curable; nevertheless, it remains the case both here and in Hades that it takes pain and torment to produce the benefit, since that is the only way in which injustice can be removed.

c   Those who act as *examples*, on the other hand, are those who have committed such awful crimes that they've become incurable. Although this means that they themselves are past help, others can be helped by watching them suffer for ever the worst, most agonizing, and most terrifying torments imaginable as a result of their sins. Their only purpose is to hang there in their prison in Hades as visible deterrents for every new criminal who arrives there.

d   If what Polus says is true,* then in my opinion Archelaus will become one of these deterrents, and he'll be joined by anyone else who's a dictator like him. In fact, I think most of those who act as examples are drawn from the ranks of dictators, kings, potentates, and politicians, because they're the ones who can and do commit the most terrible and immoral crimes. Homer testifies to this,* since in his poems those who are condemned to be punished for ever in

e   Hades are kings and potentates such as Tantalus, Sisyphus, and Tityus. However, no poet portrays Thersites (or anyone else who may have been bad, but who wasn't involved in public life) as an incurable criminal in the grip of terrible punishment, and I imagine it's because he didn't have the same scope for wrongdoing that he's better off than those who

132

did. No, Callicles, it's power that leads men to plumb the depths of depravity. 526a

All the same, there's nothing to stop good men gaining power too, and those who do deserve our wholehearted admiration, because it's not easy, Callicles, and therefore particularly commendable, to have so much opportunity for wrongdoing and yet to live a moral life. Few people manage it. I mean, there have been paragons like that both here in Athens and elsewhere, and I think more will appear in the future too, who practise the virtue of moral management of the affairs entrusted to them. In fact, one of them— Aristides the son of Lysimachus—became famous b throughout Greece, not just locally. But power usually corrupts people, my friend.

Anyway, to recapitulate, when Rhadamanthys gets hold of someone like that, he doesn't even know his name or his background; all he knows is that he's a bad man. Once he's seen this about him, he puts a token* on him to indicate whether in his opinion the person is curable or incurable, and then has him led away to Tartarus, where he undergoes the appropriate treatment. Occasionally, however, he comes across a different kind of soul, one which has lived a life of c moral integrity, and which belonged to a man who played no part in public life or—and this is the most likely possibility, in my opinion, Callicles*—to a philosopher who minded his own business and remained detached from things throughout his life. When this happens, Rhadamanthys is delighted and sends him away to the Isles of the Blessed. Aeacus goes through exactly the same procedure.* Minos sits there overseeing the whole process, and while the other two each hold a staff, he alone has a golden sceptre. That's how Homer's Odysseus saw him, 'with scep- d tre of gold, dispensing right among the dead'.*

Well, Callicles, I myself find this account persuasive, and I intend to present the judge with as healthy a soul as possible. So I'll ignore the public honours which attract most people, follow the path of truth, and try to be as moral a person as I can during my lifetime and after my death as well. I do all I can

e to recommend this course of action to others too. In particular, in response to your appeal to me, I appeal to you to take up this way of life, to engage in this struggle which, in my opinion, is as worthwhile a struggle as you'll find here in this world.* I think it's a flaw in you that you won't be able to defend yourself when the time comes for you to undergo the trial and the assessment which I've just been talking about. Instead, when you come to be judged by that son of

527a Aegina and he seizes you and takes you away, your head will spin and your mouth will gape there in that world just as much as mine would here, and the chances are that someone will smash you in the face and generally abuse you as if you were a nobody without any status at all.

You probably consider all this a ludicrous old wives' tale. There would indeed be nothing strange about despising it if we could somehow come across a better and truer account, but as it is you can see that you three—you and Polus and Gorgias, the three clever-

b est people in Greece today—have failed to prove that any other way of life is preferable to the one I've been arguing for, which also turns out to be to our advantage in the next world too. Argument after argument can be proved wrong, but just one holds its ground—that we have to take greater care to avoid doing wrong than we do to avoid suffering wrong, and that above all else we must concentrate not on making people believe that we're good, but on being good, in our private lives as well as in public. If someone does prove to be bad, however, punishment is essential, and the next best thing to actually being a moral person is becoming one—that is, learning restraint by paying the penalty for one's wrongdoing.

c Furthermore, we must have nothing to do with flattery in any of its guises—not only flattery of oneself, but

134

flattery of others too, whether they're in small groups or in a large crowd. And rhetoric (just like any other activity) should only ever be used in the service of right.

Will you be persuaded by me? You should join me on the road to a place which, our discussion suggests, holds happiness for you not only during your lifetime, but after your death as well. Let people despise you and abuse you as an idiot, if they like; yes, let them even strike you ignominiously in the face. Why should that worry you? Nothing terrible will happen to you d as long as you really are a good and moral person, training yourself in the exercise of virtue. Once we've completed our training together in this respect, then, and only then, will we turn to public life, if that seems appropriate, or to contributing ideas of ours to political debates, because by then we'll have better ideas to contribute than we do at the moment. The point is that it's embarrassing for people who are in the position we seem to find ourselves in at present to strut around as if we were important, when we're so far from understanding things that we never think the same thought twice about the same issues—and not just any old issues, but the most important ones in the world. We'd better rely on the clear light of e our recent discussion to show us the way forward, and it suggests that the exercise of justice and virtue in general is the ideal way of doing things during our lifetimes and also after our deaths. So let's take this argument as authoritative, and try to win others over to our view as well, rather than trusting in the argument you relied on when you were trying to win me over, because that one, Callicles, is good for nothing.

EXPLANATORY NOTES

447a *a number of fine pieces*: a sophistic 'display' or 'presentation' (*epideixis*) could consist of a lecture, a debate, a question-and-answer session, or a combination of these forms.

447c *conversation with us?*: 'conversation' translates a Greek word which is cognate with 'dialectic', Socrates' word for his method of philosophical enquiry, by testing the consistency of the set of one's own or others' beliefs, in order to attempt to discern the truth of some matter by forming a coherent set of notions about it under some self-evident or at least mutually agreed general proposition.

448c *the finest there is*: Polus was a historical person, a teacher of rhetoric (see Index of Names), and there can be no doubt that in this bombastic little speech, with its antitheses and reduplicated words, Plato is parodying his style (see also *Phaedrus* 267b–c). At 467b–c assonance is added to Polus' rhetorical tricks. The idea that experience leads to expertise is also alluded to at 462b–c.

449a *I avow I am*: a common Homeric formula.

450a *speaking too*: the weakness of this argument as it stands is fairly evident, and Gorgias will go on to protest (450b–c) that speech is only a secondary concern of other branches of knowledge, whereas it is the essential concern of rhetoric; however, Socrates successfully refutes that escape-route. A more profitable line for Gorgias might be that rhetoric is concerned with how to speak, rather than what is said. However, it is clear that for Gorgias rhetoric was not just a matter of the formal elements of talking—the development of a nice, persuasive style—but included enough of a general education for a speaker to be convincing about 'important' (i.e. political) matters. That is precisely why Plato was interested in attacking rhetoric and proving its nullity: it was a rival for the position held in his view by philosophy, as the only viable system of higher education.

450d *not forgetting backgammon*: because it involves counting the spaces to be moved, as well as actually moving the pieces.

451e *honest wealth*: the full text of this *skolion* (a type of popular short song) has been preserved:

> The very best thing for a person is health,
> Second good looks and third honest wealth,
> The fourth is to be in the prime of your life
> With people around you who cause you no strife.

452e *the Assembly*: the two main organs of the people in democratic Athens were the Assembly and the Council. Any male citizen over the age of eighteen had the right to attend the Assembly, which was the executive body; the Council of 500 members chosen annually by lot from the ten tribes into which citizens were divided prepared motions for the Assembly. The Athenian political system also made the lawcourts a vital tool of the democracy: any prominent political figure would be likely to find himself in court a number of times, as either a defendant or a prosecutor, or just to explain his actions during his last year of office. The jury (who also acted as judges and passed sentence) might number several hundreds, and again any male citizen over eighteen could be a juryman.

455c *not rhetoricians*: then see Socrates' assaults on certain eminent 'rhetoricians' from Athens' past at 503c–d and 515c–517c.

455e *the Middle Wall*: in the 490s, Themistocles was the statesman who was far-sighted enough to see that Athens' future lay in being a sea-power. He pushed through a programme of developing the Piraeus as a port, in addition to Phalerum, and of fortifying these two ports against invasion from the land. In the 470s, following the Greek repulse of the Persian invasion, it was again Themistocles who made sure that Athens' walls were rebuilt. His ideas were continued after his death with the construction in the 450s of the Long Walls (north and south), which stretched from Athens down to the sea, enclosing both the Piraeus and Phalerum, which lay a few miles south of the Piraeus. By the 440s, however, the role of Phalerum had been more or less entirely usurped by the Piraeus, so Pericles arranged for the building of a Middle Wall to connect Athens only to the Piraeus. The South Wall therefore fell into disuse.
   Gorgias is exaggerating if he means to imply that political decisions in Athens were always, or often, influenced

138

by rhetoricians; nevertheless, they *could* exert such influence, and that is enough for Socrates. It is one of his recurring criticisms of Athenian democracy that it relied on untrained amateurs who happened to be persuasive. On Socrates and Athenian politics, see R. Kraut, *Socrates and the State* (Princeton: Princeton University Press, 1984).

456d *pancratiast*: the pancration was a brutal combination of wrestling and boxing.

458b *discussing at the moment*: Socrates means morality; see 454b ff. Throughout Plato's dialogues, morality is repeatedly said to be the most important matter in the world to have correct views about.

459c *knows more than experts*: strictly, Gorgias has not said this. He has only said that a rhetorician is more persuasive than an expert. Socrates is assuming that his persuasiveness rests on his appearing to know more, rather than on (say) his ability to speak well.

459e *to understand any of these matters*: see 454c–455a.

460a *what rhetoric is capable of doing*: Gorgias made the promise at 455d.

460a *doesn't already know*: as Polus points out at 461b, this contradicts Gorgias' earlier disclaimer (456c–457c) to bear no responsibility for immoral use of rhetoric by his pupils. But Gorgias is worried that, if he claimed not to have the ability to teach morality, Socrates would ridicule rhetoric as amoral and therefore not a good thing.

460b *no doubt about it*: actually, it doesn't follow at all, except on the assumption that understanding a subject automatically alters a person's character and behaviour, and on the typically Socratic assumption (which there is no reason for Gorgias to share) that morality is a kind of knowledge which is analogous to other branches of knowledge. On this 'Craft Analogy', see Irwin, *Plato's Moral Theory*, ch. 3, and especially Roochnik's paper in the collection of essays edited by Benson; and for a reconstruction of a less question-begging argument, see Irwin, *Plato: Gorgias*, 126–7.

461b *I suppose*: in fact, of course, Socrates exposed or hinted at more weaknesses in Gorgias' position than simply the one Polus identifies.

461d *the beginning of this discussion*: see 448c–d.

461e *the other point of view*: Plato quotes from the comic poet Crates' lost play *Theria* (fr. 17.1 Kassel–Austin, vol. iv).

462c *recently read*: see also Polus' views as paraphrased at 448c.

462c *knack*: see also 500e–501c on knacks. The main problems with a knack, as Socrates uses the word, are (a) that it aims for pleasure rather than the good of its subject; (b) that it does not follow the dictates of a general rational theory about what is objectively good for its subject, but has learned experientially to recognize signs of its subject's pleasure. Irwin (*Plato: Gorgias*, 210) helpfully compares clothes-making, which has objective standards for good clothes (comfortable, durable, well fitting, etc.), with fashion-designing, which only tries to please the customer.

463e *young and impatient*: there is probably a pun here on Polus' name, which is also the Greek for 'colt'.

464b *justice to medicine*: the aspect of this analogy that compares physical health and psychological morality will play a considerable part in the dialogue (see 477e–479e, 504a–e, 511e–512b, 517c–519d). For discussion, see Santas, 286–303, and A. Kenny, 'Mental Health in Plato's *Republic*', in A. Kenny, *The Anatomy of the Soul* (Oxford: Basil Blackwell, 1973), 1–27.

464d *best for the body*: surely a cook is not really trying to deceive us. As elsewhere, Plato's contrast between 'pleasant' and 'good' is too extreme: sometimes good food might be pleasant food. Plato's point comes out best by contrasting a cook and a doctor when someone is ill, rather than in normal circumstances: a cook, *qua* cook, wouldn't know what diet will help to make the patient better; 'making better' is the doctor's province—i.e. the province of expertise.

464e *starvation!*: a parody of the Greek practice of trying to make the punishment fit the crime.

465c *as I say*: at 464c.

465d *would be rife*: the philosopher Anaxagoras postulated an original state of undifferentiated matter-in-potential, in which no particular quality or thing was yet distinct. The world and all its parts evolved out of this primal state. In 'everything would be jumbled up together' Plato paraphrases the first few words of Anaxagoras' treatise. A good discussion of Anaxagoras' thought may be found in G. S. Kirk, J. E. Raven, and M. Schofield, *The Presocratic Philosophers* (Cambridge: Cambridge University Press, 1983), ch. 12.

466a *branch of flattery*: Socrates' objection is unfair, since in Greek, as in English, the phrase 'to be a rhetorician is to be a flatterer' need not imply that rhetoric and flattery are entirely coextensive. Socrates himself had used the phrase in exactly that way at 464e ('cookery is ⟨a kind of⟩ flattery') and will do so again at 467a ('rhetoric is ⟨a kind of⟩ flattery').

466b *aren't they?*: the issue of power was first raised by Gorgias himself at 452d. Since the sole purpose of rhetoric is to win people over to a point of view, it is designed to bring power to its practitioners, and so 'Someone who thinks that rhetoric is an unqualified good for the rhetor must in consistency accept that power is an unqualified good' (Irwin, *Plato: Gorgias*, 138). Hence the question of power is essentially relevant to a discussion of rhetoric. On the argument that follows, in addition to items in the bibliography (including McTighe in the collection of essays edited by Benson), some valuable points are made by R. Weiss, 'Killing, Confiscating and Banishing at *Gorgias* 466–468', *Ancient Philosophy* 12 (1992), 299–315.

467a *not a kind of flattery?*: the simple conjunction of flattery and unintelligence is somewhat naïve, since it is easy to conceive of intelligent flattery (cf. Plutarch, 'How to Tell a Flatterer from a Friend', *Moralia* 48E–74E). Plato's next point is better, if he is understood as saying that the mere wielding of power is not *per se* good, as Gorgias and Polus have been claiming; there also needs to be some essential connection with benefit. However, calling rhetoricians unintelligent at this point is not a gratuitous slur: it reminds one of Gorgias' claim that rhetoricians do not need rational expertise. Then Socrates can argue that only expertise can lead you to know what is truly good for you, and therefore what you truly want; since power is defined as the ability to get what you want, then rhetoricians, *qua* unintelligent or lacking rational expertise, lack power.

467c *you might have said!*: see note on 448c.

467c *suffering*: most Greek potions were extremely bitter herbal concoctions. Note that even if the means to some end are undesirable in themselves (i.e. would be undesirable if they were ends), it seems rather unfair to say that we do not in some sense 'want' them, as if we could separate them from the end towards which they lead. It is also wrong—or at least counter-intuitive—to say that I cannot want what is bad: I do in some sense want that fifth cocktail, even though I do not want the hangover the following morning. But then Socrates notoriously denied the possibility of weakness of will: see especially *Protagoras* 352a–357e, with the commentary in C. C. W. Taylor, *Plato: Protagoras* (Oxford: Oxford University Press, 1976).

468b *want good*: it is noticeable how Plato seems for most of the argument to refuse to spell out 'good' as 'good for oneself'. It is more plausible to claim that our actions are motivated by what we perceive as good for ourselves, but Plato seems not to want to rule out some larger and more altruistic conception of good as well. See the article by F. C. White and p. xxiv above. It is also noticeable how Plato seems to restrict 'wanting' to cases where what is wanted is actually (not just apparently) best for the person doing the wanting. In other words, the argument fails to convince because it redefines the terms—especially the key terms 'want' and 'power'. An important defence of Plato's argument here is, however, mounted by Penner ('Desire and Power'). He claims that Plato is not redefining the terms of the argument so much as trying to deepen our understanding of what it is to 'want' something.

468d *doing what he wants*: the problem with the argument is that 'want' is ambiguous, in a subtle way. To use the familiar philosophical example, Oedipus wants to marry Jocasta, but he does not want to marry his own mother: one can want and not want the same thing under different descriptions. In this argument, Socrates establishes that people want good things in order to conclude that where something is bad people cannot be said to want it. But the good things that people want are things which they *suppose* to be good; the bad things that people do not want are things which are *actually* bad. The flaw in the argument lies in the shift from apparent good and bad things to actual good and bad things.

468e *to do what he wants*: The conclusion is correctly phrased
in this tentative or hypothetical manner ('might . . .'), because Socrates has only argued that *if* a person with great
political power makes a mistake about what is in his interest, *then* political power is not a good thing. He has yet
to prove that it is possible to make a mistake about what
is in one's interest, or that having your political enemies
executed (etc.) is not in one's best interest. The next phase
of the argument will cover this to some extent. Just as im-
portantly, Socrates' argument has not really dented Polus'
position because of an ambiguity within 'good'. When
Polus claims that political power is a good thing, he arguably means that it is good overall; on balance, a life with
political power is better than a life without political power.
In that case, a dictator would have to go on and on making
the kinds of mistakes Socrates is talking about for the
balance of the dictator's life to shift to being bad and to
being describable as not wanted by the dictator himself.
And finally, Socrates has conspicuously failed to prove
that a rhetorician doesn't have the power to kill others,
which was what Polus meant by power in the first place
(466b–c).

469d *armpit*: this was a common place to conceal weapons in
the days before pockets.

470d *rules Macedonia*: what is the dramatic date of the dialogue? Archelaus gained the Macedonian throne in 413
BC, but other indications point in contradictory directions.
For instance, at 519a–b Alcibiades' role in the downfall
of Athens in 415 BC is *predicted*. See Dodds, 17–18, and
his conclusion that Plato did not care about the trivia of
precise dramatic dating.

    The absolute date of composition of the dialogue can-
not be pinpointed; Plato perhaps wrote it about 385 BC. Its
relation to other dialogues—*Protagoras* in particular—is a
matter of controversy. See Irwin, *Plato: Gorgias*, 5–8, and
the debate between C. H. Kahn and M. L. McPherran in
Oxford Studies in Ancient Philosophy 6 (1988), 8 (1990),
and 9 (1991).

470e *happy either*: the happiness of the king of Persia was a
stock debating point during the fifth century in Athens.

470e *or a woman happy*: including women is a nice touch. The
term translated 'true goodness' is *kalos kagathos* which was,

until the Socratics took it over, the term for the traditional *masculine* virtues epitomized in the Athenian estate-owning gentleman.

471a *of course he does*: on Archelaus, see Index of Names. Poets and philosophers throughout the history of Greek literature wrestled with the question of how the gods could, apparently, allow a wicked person to prosper. A popular solution, for instance, was to claim that his crimes would sooner or later catch up with him, if not during his lifetime, then either through his descendants or in another incarnation. Plato's bold solution was simply to deny that a bad person is genuinely happy; precisely because, and to the extent that, he is bad, he is miserable.

471b *his master*: it was considered perfectly normal in the ancient Greek world for male slave-owners to have sex with their female slaves. The precise status of the issue of such unions in Macedon at the time is unclear. In any case, it is clear that the throne was hardly going to be his by right.

471d *early in our conversation*: 448d.

472a *in the precinct of Dionysus*: each year eminent citizens were required to act as *chorēgoi*—to fund the famous dramatic festivals of Athens. If the play a *chorēgos* had funded won the competition, he was awarded a tripod, which he then dedicated to Dionysus, who was the patron god of these dramatic festivals. Since you could be a *chorēgos* only if you were very rich, and since wealth and eminence in society tend to go together, then the fact that Nicias and his brothers (about whom we know next to nothing) have won a whole row of tripods is a sign of social eminence; the family was indeed fabulously wealthy. Moreover, Plutarch records (*Life of Nicias* 3. 3) that Nicias actually had a temple built in the precinct of Dionysus to display his tripods.

472b *Pythian Apollo*: there is some evidence that tripods awarded to a successful *chorēgos* (see previous note) at the Athenian choral festival of Thargelia could be dedicated at the precinct of Pythian Apollo in Athens. But if that is what is being referred to here, why does Plato single it out as being 'wonderful'? Why should one tripod be more wonderful than another? Since Plato singles out Aristocrates' votive offering (*anathēma*) in this way, and

144

speaks of it in conjunction with Nicias' offerings, it seems likely that Aristocrates too, like Nicias, had gone as far as having a shrine or temple built in the precinct in honour of his victory or victories. The term *anathēma* could cover dedications as small as a tripod or as large as a temple.

472b *my inheritance, the truth*: the complexities of Athenian civic law were such that it was quite common for disputes about inheritance to be settled in court. So Socrates uses this as a way of continuing his analogy with court cases and witnesses.

473a *earlier*: 469b.

473b *earlier one*: this is heavily ironic, compounding the irony of 470c.

473b *proved wrong*: Socrates would presumably accept that the truth can *seem* to be disproved, but he believes that it really survives such arguments: the fault is in the argumentational weakness of the defender of the truth, not in the truth itself. At the same time, since *Gorgias* is more self-reflective about Socrates' method of argument (see pp. xxvi–xxxii), Socrates may also be making a formal (and very bold) claim: anything that survives his elenchus may be taken to be true. See also 508e–509a.

473e *executive committee*: see note on 452e. Each of the ten tribes took turns to form the executive committee (*prutaneia*) of the Council. Of the fifty tribal members, one was chosen (again by lot) each day to chair the committee. The occasion Socrates is referring to was when he happened to be chairman. Possibly the occasion was after the naval battle of Arginusae (406 BC) when the Athenians, angry at the heavy loss of life, put eight of the military commanders on trial simultaneously on a charge of criminal negligence in failing to stop to pick up Athenian survivors. Such simultaneous trials were contrary to accepted judicial practice. Socrates was certainly on the committee at the time, but our sources are unclear as to whether or not he was actually the chairman. In any case, he seems to have protested (unsuccessfully) against the motion. In other words, as Plato would see it, this was an occasion when Socrates put into practice the ideals expressed in our dialogue, by laying his life on the line in order to do what he considered right.

474a *a short while ago*: the reference is presumably an oblique one to 472c.

474c *more contemptible*: since the predominant (see note on 468b) use of 'good' and 'bad' throughout this argument is 'good for the agent' and 'bad for the agent', then his equation of what is good with what is admirable is somewhat disturbing. It appears to deny that it is ever admirable to do anything (such as rescuing a drowning child) which may be disadvantageous to oneself. However, Socrates is in fact a 'moral egoist': he believes that what is good for me is doing good for others.

475a *admirable definition!*: in *Hippias Major*, however, a number of alternative definitions of what is admirable, or fineness, are tried out; the idea that it is usefulness and benefit occupies only 295a–297d of that dialogue. Perhaps the most promising idea which is not considered in *Gorgias* is that something is admirable if it is appropriate to its context (*Hippias Major* 293d–294e).

475d *to the alternative?*: there has been an ambiguity running through the argument which in fact invalidates it. When Polus proposes at 474c that suffering wrong is worse than doing wrong, the reader automatically takes this to mean that it is worse *for oneself*. Likewise, at the outset of the argument, the idea that doing wrong is more disgraceful also clearly means that it is more disgraceful for oneself. Socrates and Polus are weighing the factors that an agent might take into consideration when deciding a course of action: Is it worse for me to do it? Is it more disgraceful for me to do it?

However, at the start of his argument for the equivalence of 'more contemptible' and 'worse', Socrates implicitly imported the suffix *for others*, since the most natural way of taking what he says, based on 474d–475a, is that something is more contemptible if it is more unpleasant *for others* or worse *for others*. Having gained Polus' agreement to this equivalence, and since Polus has claimed from the start that doing wrong is more contemptible than suffering wrong, Socrates now claims to have refuted Polus: his claim that doing wrong is more contemptible is equivalent to the claim that it is worse than suffering wrong. But this equivalence was couched in terms of *for others*, whereas Polus' original claim was couched in terms of *for oneself*, so in fact Socrates' argument has not really affected Polus' position.

That there is a shift in the specification of who enjoys the benefit or suffers the unpleasantness or whatever is generally (but not always—Berman (below) thinks that the argument is valid) agreed by the commentators. However, there are differences in the way they analyse the fallacy in this and the subsequent arguments. In addition to works mentioned in the bibliography, the reader could profit from articles by S. Berman in *Ancient Philosophy* 11 (1991), C. N. Johnson in *Phoenix* 43 (1989), M. M. Mackenzie in *Classical Quarterly* 32 (1982), and G. Vlastos in *American Journal of Philology* 88 (1967).

477a *being benefited, then, isn't he?*: the fallacy in this argument is identical to the one in the previous argument (see preceding note). In 'a person being punished is having an admirable deed done to him', the term 'admirable' means 'admired by others'; however, Socrates translates it as 'good for the person being punished'. To put this another way: from 'punishment is a good thing', it does not necessarily follow that it is good for the person being punished.

477b *cowardice and so on*: that is, the opposites of the Greek cardinal virtues. A standard list would include morality (or, more narrowly, justice), knowledge, courage, and self-restraint (see 477d). When a few lines later, in 477c, Socrates uses 'immorality' as shorthand for lack of virtue in general, this is in keeping with the teaching of *Republic* 427e–444a that morality (or justice) is the chief virtue, which makes all the others virtues rather than mere faculties.

Socrates is now making clear what has been implicit all along. What is bad for the agent is the injustice or immorality in his mind. Even when (as in the previous argument, 474c–476a) Plato talks about *doing* wrong, his focus is implicitly on the inner state: doing wrong is an external manifestation of inner wrong, and fosters that inner wrong.

477c *property, body, and mind*: this is a recurring triad in the Platonic dialogues, and probably originated with the Pythagorean school. If Socrates' argument at this point is to have any force, the triad would have to be exhaustive.

478b *self-indulgence and injustice*: The importance, value, and flaws of Plato's apparently enlightened view that the function of punishment is to cure the imperfections in people's minds are discussed by M. M. Mackenzie, *Plato on Punishment* (Berkeley: University of California Press, 1981) and T. J. Saunders, *Plato's Penal Code* (Oxford: Oxford University Press, 1991), as well as by Irwin (*Plato: Gorgias*, 162–5, 245) and Santas (286–303). The view resurfaces during the 'myth' at the end of the book (525b ff.).

479b *is like*: this should not be taken to imply that his fault is not knowing that physical health involves having a strong heart and so on, but that he doesn't appreciate the benefits of health, and in particular that its benefits outweigh the pain of surgery. In general, Plato consistently portrays Socrates as believing that if people knew what was good for them, then they would act on it (and would also not be swayed by other, apparent goods).

480e *an enemy, for instance*: it was a standard tenet of Greek, pre-Christian ethics that you should do good to your friends and harm to your enemies. However, Socrates expresses this view here with some hesitation, and there is evidence from other dialogues that he rejected it and actually antici-pated Christianity in maintaining that it is never right to harm anyone. See especially ch. 7 of Vlastos, *Socrates*.

481b *has some use*: in order to make his paradoxical point that rhetoric should only be used to denounce one's own and one's friends' crimes, Socrates ignores perfectly moral uses such as defending an innocent person who has been wrongly accused of a crime.

481d *Demus the son of Pyrilampes*: Socrates' 'affair' with Alcibiades was notorious. It is mentioned incidentally from time to time in Plato's dialogues, and some episodes from it are given famous and extended treatment at *Symposium* 212d–222c. Homoerotic love was not regarded as abnor-mal in upper-class circles of ancient Athens; the canonical study of the topic is K. J. Dover's *Greek Homosexuality* (London: Duckworth, 1978). Callicles' two loves involve an untranslatable pun: Demus' name in Greek is exactly the word for 'populace'.

482b *divine dog of the Egyptians*: Anubis, the dog-headed god. The euphemistic oath 'By the dog' was a favourite of Socrates (though not unique to him) and occurs quite a few times in Plato's dialogues. Indeed, it has already occurred twice in *Gorgias* (at 461b and 466c), but the literal translation of Greek oaths (like a great many of their vocatives, for instance) makes for awkward English. They are best translated, usually, simply by adding emphasis to the sentence. Here, however, Socrates' mock solemnity is worth preserving.

482d *you relish*: Callicles has accurately summarized what Polus was saying at 461b–c, and has accurately claimed that both Gorgias and Polus made the mistake of lacking the courage of their convictions. On Plato's portrayal of the interlocutors as suffering embarrassment, see p. xxxiv.

482e *not on nature*: the history of the debate, which flourished in the intellectual ferment of the fifth century, about the advantages and disadvantages of man-made rules as opposed to natural law is ably summarized in Guthrie (ch. 4) and Kerferd (ch. 10). The debate took many forms, but Callicles' main complaint about convention (*nomos*) is simply that it distorts nature (*phusis*): the superior man has a natural right to power, extra wealth and so on. Plato too rejected the egalitarianism of democratic philosophy (see especially *Republic* 555b–558c); the main difference between him and Callicles will turn out to be a difference of opinion over what it is to fulfil one's potential as a human being, which for Callicles clearly means lording it over others. Compare Thrasymachus' position in the first book of *Republic*.

When Callicles analyses Socrates' defeat of Polus as due to an illegitimate changing of the terms from those of convention to those of nature, it is not clear whether Plato means us to take this as a serious analysis of the preceding argument, which seems far more complex than Callicles allows, rather than a convenient way for Callicles to introduce his pet theme. Johnson, however (see note on 475d), interprets the argument in such a way that Callicles' analysis of it in terms of nature and convention makes good sense.

483b *the majority of the human race*: Callicles' description of the majority as weak seems to me to tell conclusively against the thesis (argued by G. B. Kerferd, 'Plato's Treatment of Callicles in the *Gorgias*', *Proceedings of the Cambridge Philological Society* 200 (1974), 48–52) that Callicles is portrayed by Plato simply as a democrat. It is true, however, that he is a 'lover of the Athenian people' (481d, 513b). I think that historically he very probably was a democrat. Plato, however, is portraying him as a cynical democrat—as one who wants to manipulate the people in order to gain personal power, and who thinks that if he is a 'superior' person, he has every right to do this.

483d *on Scythia*: Xerxes' father Darius had expansionist ambitions for Persia. Among other expeditions, in about 510 BC he attacked the neighbouring Scythian territory (as described by the Greek historian Herodotus, in book 4 of his history) and in the 490s he turned his attention to Greece. Greek victory at the battle of Marathon ended this invasion, but after Darius' death in 485, Xerxes inherited his European ambitions. However, his massive invasion of Greece in 480 was equally unsuccessful, owing to an almost miraculous sequence of Greek victories against overwhelming odds. On the right of strong countries to dominate weaker ones, see Thucydides' fictional 'Melian Dialogue' (5. 85–113).

484b *where he says*: the following lines form about three-quarters of Pindar, fr. 169 Snell. It is highly likely that Pindar did not mean by 'law' the 'law of nature' which Callicles wants him to mean, but ordinary man-made law.

484c *life to it*: it will be helpful for the reader to bear in mind that the Greek term *philosophia* included not only what we might recognize as philosophy, or as an ancestor of it, but also science, mathematics, and higher education in general. (In English, the term 'philosophy' had much the same range, until 'science' was invented in the middle of the nineteenth century.) In a celebrated passage of the later dialogue *Theaetetus* (172b–177c), Plato takes up the themes of this paragraph and revels in the philosopher's lack of worldly wisdom. Callicles' attitude towards philosophy was not uncommon: the rich preferred politics and estate-management, the poor were too busy to appreciate it. It is far from clear how Callicles might have presented his overall position, which involves not only a rejection of conventional morality, but also approval of engagement in the practical and political activities of one's community. For most people, such engagement would go hand in hand with accepting, not rejecting, conventional morality; and Callicles too repeatedly expresses approval of the conventional accolade of being highly regarded within one's community.

484e *happens to excel*: Euripides, fr. 183 Nauck², from the lost play *Antiope*. At 485e we are told that the character Zethus spoke the lines to Amphion. There are constant echoes and quotations of this play in the next few paragraphs (see following notes): the extent of Plato's debt to the play has been discussed by A. W. Nightingale, 'Plato's *Gorgias* and Euripides' *Antiope*: A Study in Generic Transformation', *Classical Antiquity* 11 (1992), 121–41.

485d *earns distinction*: *Iliad* 9.441. The agora was the political and commercial heart of the city.

485e *and say*: Plato adapts in prose a few lines from the play (see note on 484e). He borrows quite a few words from the play, but any reconstruction of the original lines must be to some extent speculative. Another source gives us another line, and the fragment (fr. 185 Nauck², but see also Dodds's notes *ad loc.*) may originally have read as follows: 'Amphion, you're neglecting matters you should pay attention to. Look at the noble temperament with which nature has endowed you! Yet what you're famous for is behaving like a woman. You couldn't deliver a speech to the councils which adminster justice, or make a plausible and persuasive appeal . . . or join battle with an opponent bearing a hollow shield, or put passion into a proposal designed to help others.' Zethus makes an excellent spokesman for Callicles: the chief connection between Callicles' disparate recommendations (not to follow conventional morality, not to take philosophy seriously, and to engage in public life) is that he denigrates taking what he sees as a passive role in anything.

486b *and ruin him*: although unannounced, the words scan and there is no doubt that Callicles is continuing to quote from Euripides' *Antiope*. The two lines form fr. 186 Nauck².

486c *in a deserted house*: the words and phrases in quotation marks come again come from Euripides' *Antiope* (fr. 188 Nauck²), but in the original—of which we have from other sources considerably more than Plato quotes here—Zethus is telling Amphion off for his effeminate musical interests.

486d *touch my mind to it*: in ancient times gold was rubbed against a 'touchstone'—a type of black quartz on which different qualities of gold left sufficiently different marks for an expert to assay the gold.

486e *these beliefs are true*: this claim, which is repeated at 487e, is on the face of it extraordinary. Why should Socrates claim that if he and Callicles agree to an idea, that idea is true? For further discussion see pp. xxvi–xxxii, and for a reading list see section H of the Select Bibliography.

489a *someone with insight*: this paragraph has been cited as evidence that Socrates (as opposed to Plato—see note on 482e) approved of democratic egalitarianism. However, Socrates is engaged in the dialectical refutation of Callicles: he is turning his own premisses and admissions against him, rather than importing his own views.

489b *nature endorses these views too*: unfortunately, the argument is invalid as a response to Callicles, since Callicles had never claimed that natural justice consists in the legislations or assertions of the stronger party, only that it consists in the stronger party having more than, and ruling over, the weaker party. Plato seeds Socrates' counter-argument by having Callicles agree at 488d (presumably as an extension of the idea of 'ruling') that in a democracy the stronger majority are the lawmakers. In his original statement, however, at 483b, Callicles had claimed that lawmaking was a tool of the weaker party, and that natural justice and man-made law never coincide. Nevertheless, Plato does need to rule out the notion of physical strength or mere ability to enforce one's whims, and despite its invalidity as a counter-argument to Callicles' original position, the argument does successfully rule out this notion.

489b *at your age*: superficial verbal argument was thought in ancient Greek times, as now, to be above all a teenage phenomenon.

489c *physical strength at their disposal*: actually, not only did Callicles assert that 'superior' meant 'stronger' just a moment ago at 488d, but his examples of natural right at 483d–e all involved dominance by brute strength. Socrates is not here forcing him to clarify his position, then, so much as to alter it. Callicles denies that the democratic mob's views can constitute law in the sense of 'natural law'; he has already accepted at 483b–c that they do constitute man-made law. One of the common charges brought against man-made law by supporters of nature in the fifth century was that man-made rules were made and repealed at the whim of fickle and fallible humans; from this point of view the search for natural law is idealistic. Notice, then, how Callicles' position is shifting from realism to idealism—from 'natural right is what happens in spite of people's attempts to stop it happening' to 'natural right is what ought to happen'. This is particularly noticeable in the claim that it is natural right for a single intelligent person to rule over unintelligent people.

489e *keeping something back*: Socrates ironically means that Callicles was keeping back what he really meant (see previous note). Zethus was not a god, but his name is close enough to Zeus' for Socrates to bring in the joke about Callicles invoking Zethus as if he were a god.

491d *only others?*: is the issue of self-control a complete change of direction? Not quite, because since self-control was conventionally recognized as a virtue, Callicles' rejection of conventional morality raises the question. It is also fair to ask whether Callicles' superior men might not have to exercise some self-control either on their way to the top, or in order to maintain their position there. Moreover, Callicles clearly thinks that his superior man is some kind of ideal, so it is fair for Socrates to ask whether total self-indulgence can play any part in an ideal life. And finally, 'The shift from political rule to self-rule reminds us that the fundamental issue of the dialogue is moral rather than political' (Kahn, 103).

491e *arise within oneself*: Socrates' talk of controlling desires has been taken to anticipate Plato's maturer teaching in *Republic* that there are, so to speak, different parts of the mind which can conflict, and that the irrational, desiring part does not appreciate what is good for the agent, but can still override the rational part which does have such understanding. But if Plato is here pre-empting *Republic*, there is a serious clash with other passages in *Gorgias* (e.g. 468a–b, 509d–e) where in the background is the standard Socratic intellectualist doctrine that no one ever acts contrary to what he thinks it is best for him to do. In fact, however, there is no real clash. We can understand that Socrates accepts that every desire is desire for an assumed good, but also believes that no desire should be allowed to grow so strong that it threatens the agent's perception of where his overall good lies. This idea of control is all Socrates needs to argue against Callicles; we do not need to import the notion of a rational part of the mind controlling an irrational part. See J. Cooper, 'The *Gorgias* and Irwin's Socrates', *Review of Metaphysics* 35 (1981–2), 577–87.

491e *enslavement to anyone*: Callicles thinks of self-control as enslavement to oneself; Socrates will argue, on the other hand, that to give free rein to desire is to make it one's master.

492a *can grow no larger*: why, under Socrates' prodding, does Callicles allow his initially more moderate position to be escalated until he refuses to accept the value of any restraint at all on a person's desire and identifies himself in various ways as an out-and-out hedonist. Initially, for instance, he claims only that pleasure is good, not that all pleasure is good. The reasons for Plato's escalation of Callicles' position are discussed by G. Klosko, 'The Refutation of Callicles in Plato's *Gorgias*', *Greece & Rome* 31 (1984), 126–39. He concludes that it was germane to Plato's strategy to have Socrates take on the kind of hedonist who was devoted to short-term physical satisfaction. The claim of this kind of hedonism to constitute the good life had to be ruled out. The precise kind of hedonism Callicles espouses is discussed by G. Rudebusch, 'Callicles' Hedonism', *Ancient Philosophy* 12 (1992), 53–71; however, his analysis is perhaps too sophisticated for the simpler categories of our dialogue. The paper by N. P. White is better in this respect. The best work on the strategy of Socrates' argument with Callicles is that of Berman.

492a *earlier*: 483b ff.

492b *a dictator, for example*: the word translated 'dictator' here and elsewhere in the dialogue is *turannos*. *Turannoi* were certainly autocrats, but in Greek history a number of them ruled with popular acclaim and perfectly moderately; they were not necessarily vicious despots. Therefore it is clear that Plato is having Callicles espouse a *type* of person—a type who uses his autocratic power to satisfy his personal whims. This is the dictatorial type of *Republic* 571a–576b.

492e *death life*: these notorious lines from Euripides' lost play
Phrixus (fr. 639 Nauck²) were often quoted and parodied
in antiquity.

493a *the body is a tomb*: this famous notion is far more neatly
expressed in Greek: *sōma sēma*. The pun, as well as the
idea, may well have originated in the Pythagorean school,
and Pythagoreans were also probably instrumental in taking the myth of the Danaids, who were condemned (for
the crime of killing their husbands on their wedding night)
endlessly to carry water in sieves in Hades, and converting
it to allegorical use. The Greeks in general, and the esoteric schools in particular, were fond of puns and etymolo-
gies, on which they placed a lot of significance. See also
the next note. On the provenance of the mythical elements
in Plato's account here, see Dodds, 296–8; on the interpretation of the passage, see D. Blank, 'The Fate of the
Ignorant in Plato's *Gorgias*', *Hermes* 119 (1991), 22–36.

493a *plausible and persuasive*: that is, hard to resist. The Pythagorean story-teller (the main centres of Pythagoreanism in
the fifth and fourth centuries BC were Sicily and southern
Italy) is punning, but the puns cannot be translated
smoothly. 'Jar' translates *pithos*, while 'plausible' is *pith-
anos*. The next words are a double pun: there is not only
a loose pun between 'fools' (*anoētoi*) and 'non-initiates'
(*amuētoi*), but *amuētoi* could also mean 'unstoppered', as
if initiation into the Pythagorean mysteries put a stopper
on your jar. Finally, the pun that follows a couple of lines
later between 'Hades' and 'unseen' (*aïdes*) was a standard,
less esoteric piece of Greek etymology.

493b *uncapped state*: for the image, see the previous note about
'unstoppered'. The Greek is difficult, but I see no reason
to change the transmitted text, so here I prefer the reading
of editors such as Burnet and Croiset to that of Dodds.

493b *unseen*: for the pun in the Greek here, see the second note
on 493a. By interpreting 'Hades' as 'the unseen world',
Plato—or his source—transfers its inhabitants to our familiar world. Pleasures and desires are invisible; in so far
as we are subject to these and other unseen influences, we
are members of that unseen world. But Plato also believes,
as the myth at the end of our dialogue shows, that the way
of life Callicles is recommending would lead to a miserable afterlife too.

494a *feel pleasure*: Callicles is surely right to shift the emphasis
of the discussion on to pleasure, since a self-indulgent
person does not, or does not just, seek the state of satisfaction (the state of full jars), which Socrates is suggesting
is the ideal, but also, and perhaps primarily, the pleasure
of the process of satisfying a need. Plato's assumptions
and arguments about pleasure in *Gorgias* are well analysed in Gosling and Taylor's book. In particular, they
point out that even if the anti-hedonist arguments of
Gorgias were effective against a thesis that the good life
consists of a life of unending immediate (bodily) pleasures,
they do little to damage the hedonistic thesis that a life of
overall and long-term pleasure is the good life.

494b *gully-bird*: the identification of the Greek bird *charadrios*
is not entirely certain. In any case, the point is clear: it was
famous either for excreting while it eats, or perhaps for
straining water through its beak.

495a *good and bad pleasures?*: in accusing Callicles of failing
to distinguish between good and bad pleasures, Socrates is
tacitly importing some external criterion of goodness; otherwise Callicles could easily grade pleasures according to
how much pleasure they give, and call those which give
more enjoyment 'better' than those which give less.

495a *original promise*: his promise of candour, presumably.

495c *a short while ago*: 491b.

495c *separate qualities, surely?*: whereas Socrates thinks that they
are fundamentally identical: see note on 507c.

495d *Callicles of Acharnae*: Socrates is clearly trying to sound
like an official decree. Acharnae and (a couple of lines
later) Alopece were Athenian demes; demes were districts
of Athens and the surrounding territory of Attica. Every
citizen was enrolled into a particular deme for life, whether
or not he actually lived there: it depended on where his
ancestor had lived when the system was formalized under
Cleisthenes in about 505 BC.

496e *at the same time*: this contentious analysis of pleasure as
including a component of pain or distress was adhered to
by Plato throughout his life, and underlies his description
of most pleasures as 'mixed', 'impure', and 'unreal' in
Republic and *Philebus*. It is impossible to tell from *Gorgias*,

however, whether Plato thinks that all pleasures or merely most pleasures have a perceivable unpleasant component. In order to refute Callicles' identification of 'pleasant' and 'good', he only needs to show that some pleasures involve distress (which Callicles must describe as 'bad') in this way; nevertheless, the argument reads like a generalization, as if Plato wanted us to understand that pleasure always involves distress in this way.

What is important about the analysis of pleasure in *Gorgias* is the deficiency model. Pleasure is the satisfaction or replenishment (*plērōsis*) of a need or lack. This is the first clear exposition of the idea, and it is precisely this idea which enables him later to distinguish between good and bad pleasures. Even if all pleasures remedy some distress, nevertheless in the case of a few refined (largely non-bodily) pleasures, the distress might for some reason be so slight as to be imperceptible, and therefore these pleasures are pure and acceptable. Moreover, the idea that most pleasures are remedial of distress lies at the core of the way Plato refutes hedonism time and again in the dialogues: in order to maximize his pleasure, a hedonist has to maximize the distress which the pleasure is to remedy; but distress is for a hedonist bad; therefore hedonism is inane and self-contradictory.

There are grounds for dispute. First, has Plato established that a thirsty person who is drinking is really feeling simultaneous distress and pleasure in a strong enough sense? Perhaps he is only feeling distress in one respect and pleasure in another. Second, the assumption that all desires are unpleasant is unconvincing (think of the pleasurable anticipation of dinner, or of sexual arousal).

496e *the mind or the body*: it doesn't make any difference to this particular argument, perhaps, but elsewhere (e.g. *Phaedo* 65a, *Philebus* 35c) Plato is sure that the body is in itself a lump of insensate matter, and that all sensations and feelings (as well as thoughts etc.) are to be attributed to the mind.

497c *lower ones*: the major festival of the Eleusinian mysteries could not be attended unless one had also celebrated at the minor festival a few months earlier. The analogy is of great philosophical interest. Socrates is not just saying what he has said before—that his method of cross-examination is the best method he knows for getting to the truth—but is adding that the 'truth' it arrives at may in some sense fall short of the full truth. On Socrates' elenchus—his method of questioning—see pp. xxvi–xxxii; on the particular issue of the two grades of truth see pp. xxx–xxxi.

498d *doesn't it?*: The problem with this argument lies in Plato's substitution of 'pleasant' for 'good'. Even if a hedonist were to accept such a simplistic substitution, he need not follow Plato into equating the 'good' of good personal qualities with the 'good' of pleasure. See further Tenkku, 77–87.

499b *better and worse pleasures?*: but whatever criterion Callicles uses to make this distinction, he is going to have to admit the value, at least to some extent, of at least some of conventional morality. For instance, he may have to practise self-control in order to secure 'better' pleasures rather than 'worse' ones.

499c *it's so dishonest!*: actually it is not clear that Callicles needs the absolute identity of 'good' and 'pleasant', such that all and only pleasures are good: Socrates may have foisted this view on him. See the first note on 492a.

499e *you may remember*: Socrates is referring to 467e–468c.

500a *take an expert?*: the introduction of this expert is rather abrupt. We are surely competent to judge the 'good' pleasure of a cliff walk, or the 'bad' pleasure of *Schadenfreude* without any particular expertise. But Plato is thinking more of the fact that if good pleasures are a means to the good, then the good is not always immediately apparent, but lies in the future, so that it might take expertise to discern the route to it.

500a *you may remember*: the reference this time is to 462b–465d.

501c *left incomplete*: Callicles is referring to 497b.

501e *in competitions*: the *kithara* was a large lyre, favoured by professional musicians rather than for domestic enjoyment. The mention of public competitions is only intended to remind us that Plato is talking about charming large numbers of people at once, I think, rather than suggesting that there is anything particularly bad about taking part in such competitions.

501e *you've composed?*: dithyrambic poetry was a type of lyric poetry which was popular in the fifth century. Choirs were trained to sing the poet's compositions at public festivals of Dionysus.

502b *designed for?*: Plato's contempt for the low moral tone of tragedy might strike us as surprising, since we nowadays find many of the surviving Greek tragedies morally edifying. But we should counterbalance this by remembering that we read the tragedies in isolation. In ancient Athens, however, they were intended to be performed only once, in a competition; they therefore had to please the audience (or at least the judges) if they were to win the competition. This section of *Gorgias* anticipates the more developed and sophisticated condemnation of poetry in *Republic*.

503c *heard him speak*: Socrates claimed to have done so at 455e. See as usual the Index of Names for brief biographical notes on the four men named. They were the four most revered statesmen of the fifth century, and to criticize them as Plato is about to (and then see also 515b ff.) would have been as shocking a piece of iconoclasm as for a British writer today to criticize Winston Churchill.

504a *not long ago*: 452a–b, 464b ff.

504b *no choice*: actually, there is plenty of choice, of course. The argument has relied on cases of things which are both material and composite; we need an argument to convince us that the mind is composite, at least, or is composite in the requisite sense.

504d *expert of ours*: such a person represents an ideal statesman. Since his work involves restraining people's desires, presumably against their will, or at least against where they think their own good lies, then this line of thought leads directly to the political proposals of *Republic*. The medical metaphor of 505a and elsewhere also encouraged Plato's authoritarian side, since it does make some sense to suggest that a medical expert can overrrule his patients' desires, on the grounds that he knows best what is good for them. At 517b there is an overt mention of 'forcing'.

504d *giving or taking*: a politician in the Athenian mould would be expected to impose some form of taxation on the rich, and pay citizens for their attendance in one of the lawcourts.

505d *go around headless*: the meaning of the saying is clear, although its origin is obscure.

505e *to say before*: Epicharmus, fr. 16 Diels–Kranz.

506b *with Amphion's*: at 484e ff., Callicles made liberal use of Zethus' attack, in Euripides' *Antiope*, on the unworldliness of his brother Amphion's way of life; it seems likely that Amphion's response, the text of which has not survived, defended such a lifestyle.

507b *religious person*: at first sight, this sounds as though Socrates is saying that the performance of certain actions constitute justice and so on, which would clash with his constant doctrine that all the virtues are to be analysed in terms of knowledge. But the sentence can equally be read as meaning that genuinely just action can come only from someone with the knowledge which is justice.

507c *paradigm of goodness*: because he possesses the four Greek cardinal virtues. As particularly the dialogue *Protagoras* shows, Plato believes that all the virtues are in some sense one, united by the fact that they all require knowledge of what is good for oneself.

507c *well and successfully*: why is a good person bound to do things well and successfully? The most charitable interpretation has Plato simply meaning 'do well' to stand for 'act in such a way as to guarantee happiness'. Less charitably, Plato might be equivocating on 'good' (as 'expert' or 'morally good') and/or on 'do well' (as 'be successful' or 'do things morally well').

508a *unruly shambles*: the 'wise men' referred to are usually identified as Pythagoreans, since the word *kosmos* ('ordered whole') was probably first applied to the universe by them. But it is likely that Plato has in mind a variety of thinkers. Among the pre-Socratics, for instance, Anaximander and Heraclitus certainly stressed the principle of justice in the universe, and Empedocles elevated love to a cosmic principle. And it is in general true to say that all the pre-Socratics perceived the universe as in some sense an ordered whole.

508a *geometrical equality*: this ●the kind of 'equality' found in a geometrical proportion, where 2 : 4 = 4 : 8 = 8 : 16. In other words, the kind of equality Plato favours is not absolute equality, where everyone gets the same regardless of character or talent, but the kind where what people have accords with their abilities or (with greater social conscience) with what they can contribute to society. Again, this idea adumbrates much of the social thinking of *Republic*. However, since Callicles contrasted his ideal of the strong tyrant with absolute equality, Plato urgently needs to spell out how his 'geometrical equality' differs from Callicles' recommendation.

508b *used for*: Socrates made these claims at 480a–481b, at which point Callicles asked him if he was serious.

508c *fault me*: at 486a–c.

509a *iron and adamant*: 'adamant' was the word used by the Greeks to describe the hardest substance they knew. Confusingly, however, it seems to refer to more than one substance: sometimes it is described as clear (diamond?), but sometimes as dark and opaque (steel?). In apologizing for his 'extravagance', Socrates mimics Callicles at 486c, just as he will shortly echo Callicles' use of 'ridiculous' at 484e–485a.

509a *cannot fail to be wrong*: notice again Socrates' extraordinary confidence in his method of argument. See pp. xxvi–xxxii.

509e *earlier stage of the discussion*: 474b–475e.

510c *the same goes*: reading οὕτως (Schanz).

511e *Pontus*: a country at the eastern end of the south coast of the Black Sea, about 750 miles from Athens. Egypt is about 600 miles in a direct line, but in ancient times ships tended to hug coastlines rather than venture too much across the open sea. Aegina is an island a few miles southwest of Athens. An obol was an average daily wage for a labourer, and 6 obols made 1 drachma.

512b *whole cities*: that is, when they construct devices for defensive or offensive use in warfare.

513a *hold most dear*: charming the moon down from the sky (i.e. causing an eclipse) was commonly attributed to witches, but witches were also supposed to pay for their powers by losing some precious faculty such as eyesight. Thessaly comprised a large area of northern Greece; it remained relatively uncivilized for longer than much of Greece, and was regarded as one of the traditional homes of primitive arts such as magic.

513b *Demus as well*: see note on 481d.

513d *our agreement*: at 500b ff.

513e *earlier*: 504e–505b.

515a *for not doing so*: see 485c–486d.

515c *a short while ago*: 503b ff.

515e *and mercenary*: under Pericles, any Athenian citizen became eligible for a daily wage if he was empanelled as a juror in one of the lawcourts (remember that juries could number in the hundreds), if he attended the Council, and if he served in the army. This was to compensate him for loss of earnings through regular work. Here Plato reels off a list of stock charges, which probably originated among right-wing opponents of the policy. This is the point of Callicles' response: people get 'mangled ears' from boxing, which was supposed to be a peculiarly Spartan sport, so that people at Athens who took up boxing as a form of exercise were considered to be pro-Spartan—which is to say, pro-oligarchy and anti-democracy.

516a *Pericles a bad man*: a fair question, we might think. It is inconsistent of Plato to accuse the Athenian people of being fickle (as he often does) and yet to use their treatment of Pericles as evidence of his character. Perhaps his point is just that they remained fickle, and that Pericles had not succeeded in improving them in that respect. But again, lack of success in something like this should not be taken as a sign of character.

Pericles was convicted of embezzlement in 430 BC or thereabouts, and had to pay a heavy fine. Thucydides (2. 65) attributes the charge to general ill will against Pericles because of the hardship of war. He mentions what Plato conveniently fails to mention—that Pericles was reinstated in 429, soon after the trial (although he died a few months later).

516c *Homer says*: several times in the *Odyssey* (6. 120, 9. 175, 13. 201) Homer uses the formulaic phrase 'wild [or fierce] and immoral'.

516d *exile as well*: once a year, the Athenian people had the right to ostracize a leading statesman, if they disapproved of his policies and treatment of them. If they decided to conduct an ostracism (which they didn't every year, and the practice gradually fell into disuse through the fifth century, after a rash of ostracisms in the 480s), then an extraordinary Assembly was held. A minimum of 6,000 votes had to be cast for the ostracism to be valid; the politician whose name was most often inscribed on the sherds (*ostraka*) was banished from the city for ten years (though he could be recalled within that period). Ostracism was a sign of political failure, but was not a punishment, and its victim was allowed to retain all his property and rights. Exile, however, was a punishment for criminal activity; its victim was stripped of his rights and, unless commuted, the sentence was for life.

516e   *carried out*: for the 'executive committee', see note on 473e. The 'pit' was a place of execution, just outside Athens, which was reserved particularly for political criminals.

516e   *earlier*: 503a–d.

517c   *and so on and so forth*: it is surely stretching the point to claim that in providing Athens with these things, the statesmen were pandering to the masses. Themistocles' proposal to strengthen the navy actually had to compete with an alternative proposal to distribute among the citizen body the money he wanted to spend on building a navy. The exaggerated nature of Plato's criticism of these leading statesmen is often attributed to personal bitterness; I suspect that he felt they had wasted golden opportunities. Throughout his life Plato was tempted by the idea that a suitable political system could somehow help instil moral goodness in its citizens. Plato possibly believed, then, that instead of spending their time with fortifications and navies, Themistocles and the others should have exerted themselves to found the ideal state. There may also be an underlying intuition that these demagogues flattered the Athenian people into believing that they, the people, were the true leaders, when they were actually being led.

It is relevant to remember that the attack on politicians is not a gratuitous digression. The ostensible target of Plato's scorn throughout the dialogue is rhetoric and its ramifications, and rhetoric was central to Athenian politics at the time. These politicians were ensnared, in Plato's opinion, by the superficial goals of the outer life.

518a *degrading*: compare the terms of Callicles' denigration of philosophy at 485b–c.

519a *as well*: Alcibiades was notoriously blamed for at least some of Athens' setbacks during the Peloponnesian War, so Plato's point here is extremely contentious. He is saying that the real blame lies with the famous four statesmen of the past.

519e *professional teachers of goodness*: the sophists. Socrates' tone is sarcastic. The 'goodness' or 'virtue' they offered to teach commonly meant how to be successful in politics. Callicles' contempt for the sophists was probably the majority view, though they were enthusiastically welcomed in some quarters. It was contempt born of fear, just as thinkers on the fringe are feared in all ages.

520a *suggested to Polus*: at 465c.

521b *cast aspersions*: literally, 'call it a Mysian'. The Mysians (from north-west Asia Minor) were proverbially contemptible.

521d *true statesman*: Plato's *Republic* is in essence a thorough elaboration of the connection between moral knowledge and political expertise.

521e *the subtle route*: Callicles had used the Euripidean phrase at 486c to denigrate Socratic argument; here Socrates turns it against rhetoric.

521e *talking to Polus*: at 464d–e.

521e *the youngest among you*: since the children the cook is addressing stand for the Athenian people as a whole, then the youngest children stand for the Athenian youth. This is a parody of one of the actual charges against Socrates in 399; he was accused of 'ruining [or corrupting] the young' (see 522b–c). The full charge included religious nonconformism as well. The 'bafflement' which Socrates produced in his interlocutors was the result of showing them the error of blind adherence to their conditioned moral views; this could be, and was, superficially interpreted as an attempt to undermine the prevailing moral code.

522e *soul*: it is important for the reader to be aware that the same word will be translated 'soul' in what follows as has been consistently translated 'mind' throughout the rest of

164

the dialogue. The Greek concept of *psukhē* was capacious: it was at once the life-force, *and* that which receives impressions, stores knowledge, and does all the things we think of the mind as doing, *and* (for those who believed in such things) was also liable to an afterlife, and even reincarnation. It is rather closer to the Buddhist concept of 'mind', then, than the usual Western one.

523a *the truth*: the 'myth' that follows may be compared with Plato's other eschatological myths at the end of *Phaedo* and *Republic* (and see also *Phaedrus* 246a ff.). As usual, Plato interweaves his own invention with folk tradition and mystical elements drawn from Pythagoreanism and Orphism. On these myths, see J. Annas, 'Plato's Myths of Judgement', *Phronesis* 27 (1982), 119–43.

523a *between themselves*: Homer, *Iliad* 15. 187–93.

523b *Tartarus*: this was traditionally the lowest and most hellish part of the underworld, reserved for special criminals. The Isles of the Blessed were naturally described differently according to the predilections of the describer.

524a *Tartarus respectively*: the meadow first appears as the asphodel meadow of Homer's *Odyssey* 11. 539, and became a regular feature of the geography of the underworld. Some kind of crossroads is also a standard feature, at any rate where afterlife judgement is involved, because it is of course a topographical representation of judgement. See especially *Republic* 614c.

524a *from Europe*: it was commonly believed among the Greeks that there were only these two continents. They knew the northern African coast, but included it in one or the other of the two continents.

525b *to improve*: in the underworld, the dead can see other souls being punished, and this will help them to improve when they come to be reincarnated. Plato does not here express the doctrine of reincarnation which features in later dialogues, but his theory only makes sense in the context of such a doctrine. The idea that some people are incurably bad, and are punished only to deter others from committing crimes, sits awkwardly with the insistence at 472e and elsewhere that punishment is always good for the criminal. Perhaps Plato assumes that we can only count someone as incurable after his death.

525d *what Polus says is true*: 470d ff.

525d *Homer testifies to this*: *Odyssey* 11. 572–600.

526b *token*: similar tokens appear at *Republic* 614c.

526c *Callicles*: remember Callicles' contempt for philosophy at 484c ff.

526c *same procedure*: that is, with those from Europe (523e–524a).

526d *among the dead*: *Odyssey* 11. 569.

526e *in this world*: there are plenty of echoes in Socrates' words here of Callicles at 483b and 486a–c, especially.

INDEX OF NAMES

AEACUS: son of Zeus and Aegina, the eponymous nymph of the island near Athens, on which Aeacus lived. He was famous for his piety, for being Achilles' grandfather, and for becoming one of the judges of the underworld. Plato is the first to name these judges, at *Apology* 41a.

ALCETAS: Alcetas (along with Alexander, Perdiccas, and Philip) are common names in the Macedonian royal family. This one was the brother of Perdiccas II (q.v.). On Perdiccas' death, Alcetas could have gained the throne, but he and his son Alexander were killed by Archelaus (q.v.) as rivals to his own dynastic ambitions.

ALCIBIADES: 452–404 BC. A talented statesman and military tactician with immense wealth and personal charisma, who squandered all this potential by scandalous personal behaviour and oligarchic political associations. Exiled in 415 BC, when he was about to take command of Athens' do-or-die expedition to Sicily, he went over to Athens' enemies, before becoming a kind of overlord in Thrace and allying himself once more with Athens. His reinstatement in Athens in 407 was shortlived, and he soon fled to his northern territories, where he was assassinated by agents of the Persian king. His friendship with Socrates is vividly portrayed in Plato's *Symposium*.

ALEXANDER: son of Alcetas (q.v.), murdered by Archelaus (q.v.).

AMPHION: son of Antiope and Zeus, and brother of Zethus. He was a legendary musician, and in Euripides' *Antiope* (performed *c*.410 BC) he represented the passive virtues of culture and contemplation, while his brother represented ambition and political involvement.

ANAXAGORAS: *c*.500–428 BC, from Clazomenae. One of the most complex and significant of the pre-Socratic philosophers or proto-scientists. His work was well known in Athens, where he stayed for some years and was a personal friend of Pericles.

ANDRON: a friend of Callicles. A member of the moderate oligarchic government of Four Hundred in 411 BC, he turned informant to save his skin when the oligarchy collapsed.

APOLLO: god of disease, medicine, music, reason, civilization, and prophecy. Delphi, in the district of Pytho, was sacred to him as the god of prophecy.

ARCHELAUS: king of Macedon 413–399 BC. He continued the unifying work of his predecessor Perdiccas II (q.v.), and was also famous as a patron of the arts: Euripides and Agathon, the tragedians, accepted invitations to his court, for instance. He apparently also issued such an invitation to Socrates (Aristotle, *Rhetoric* 1398ª24), but Socrates refused. He was, at least for a while, a valued ally of Athens. In painting him as the type of immorality, then, Plato is justifying Socrates' judgement over that of Athens.

ARISTIDES: *c.*530–465 BC. Athenian statesman, named 'the Just'. Active during the Persian Wars, and a political rival of Themistocles, as a result of which he was ostracized in 482, but recalled two years later when Athens was faced with the threat of Xerxes (q.v.). Popular Athenian stories painted Themistocles as wily and Aristides as honest; this seems to be the background of Socrates' approbation at 526b.

ARISTOCRATES: a member of the short-lived oligarchic government of the Four Hundred in Athens in 411 BC, and one of the generals at the battle of Arginusae in 406. Otherwise, little is known about him; the context of his mention at 472a–b testifies to his wealth and (Plato suggests) to his respect for wealth and power.

ARISTOPHON: one of a famous Athenian family of painters; both he and his father Aglaophon were eclipsed by the fame of his brother Polygnotus.

CALLICLES: unknown outside *Gorgias*, but surely a historical person, rather than a Platonic fiction, since Plato tells us about his love for Demus (481d–e, 513b), and names his deme (495d) and three of his friends (487c). He may well have died young, and therefore left no further traces in the historical record. Nevertheless, Plato uses him as a type: he is a conventionally educated young Athenian aristocrat who has been influenced enough by the new ideas current at the end of the fifth century to be a spokesman for a materialistic and hedonistic personal philosophy. See also note on 483b.

CHAEREPHON: an old friend and follower of Socrates, who appears from time to time in Plato's dialogues in minor roles, but is particularly famous as the instigator of the Delphic oracle which pronounced Socrates the wisest man alive (*Apology* 21a).

CIMON: *c.*510–449 BC. Athenian statesman and military commander, and son of Miltiades (q.v.). Very successful as a conservative in domestic politics and as a bold strategist in military campaigns particularly in the 470s and early 460s; a political rival of Themistocles (q.v.) and later Pericles (q.v.).

CINESIAS: fl. *c.*420 BC. A notoriously bad dithyrambic poet much mocked in the plays of Old Comedians, such as Aristophanes, for his ugliness as well as for his tasteless musical innovations.

CLEOPATRA: otherwise unknown wife of Perdiccas II of Macedonia (q.v.).

CRONUS: father of Zeus and chief deity before Zeus took over. The time of his reign therefore represents the dim, distant past, whether that was seen as a brutal or a golden age.

DEMUS: A famously attractive young man of the time. Dodds's note on 481d5 is definitive.

DIONYSUS: god of mystic ecstasy, fertile growth, and dramatic festivals.

EPICHARMUS: fl. *c.*480 BC. Sicilian comic playwright, much favoured by later philosophers for his pithy maxims. Few fragments of his works remain.

EURIPIDES: *c.*485–406 BC; with Aeschylus and Sophocles, one of the three great tragedians of Athens' golden period.

GERYON: see Heracles.

GORGIAS: *c.*480–376 BC, from Leontini in Sicily; one of the giants of the sophistic movement, and a well-known figure in Athens. He specialized not in philosophy, but in the budding art of rhetoric, in which he was a great innovator; although much of his style seems horribly artificial to us today, it seems to have dazzled his contemporaries. 'Starting with the initial advantage of having nothing in particular to say, he was able to concentrate all his energies upon saying it' (J. D. Denniston, *Greek Prose Style* (London: Oxford University Press, 1952), 12).

HERACLES: the great hero of Greek legend, famous for his twelve labours and an important figure in numerous other tales. He also had a thriving cult throughout Greece. In one of his labours, he had to steal the magnificent cattle of Geryon, the three-headed ruler of Erytheia, and drive them all the way back to Eurystheus in Greece. He succeeded, after many adventures and plenty of slaughter.

HERODICUS: Gorgias' brother, an otherwise virtually unknown doctor.

HOMER: fl. *c.*750 BC. The greatest epic poet of Greece; his *Iliad* sings of the death and glory of the Trojan War, while his *Odyssey* recounts the fanciful and marvellous adventures of one hero, Odysseus, returning from the war.

MELES: apparently as bad a composer and player of *kithara* music as his son Cinesias (q.v.) was of dithyrambic poetry and music.

MILTIADES: *c.*550–489 BC. Athenian noble who acted as puppet ruler of Thrace for many years, until returning to Athens in time to become an influential statesman and to win undying fame as the 'hero of Marathon', where in 490 he defeated the Persian invaders against all the odds.

MINOS: legendary king of Crete, and builder of the labyrinth. The son of Zeus and Europa, he was credited with establishing a good legal code in Crete, which is presumably what entitles him to become a judge in the underworld. One of the other judges, Rhadamanthys, was his brother.

MITHAECUS: a famous cook.

NAUSICYDES: An Athenian miller who seems to have cornered enough of the market to charge high prices and make himself a fortune. Athens' grain supply was always precarious, so prices could rise a great deal.

NICIAS: *c.*470–413 BC. Most famous as the Athenian general whose faltering doomed the disastrous Sicilian expedition of 415. He was a political moderate, as well as an unadventurous commander. He came from an incredibly wealthy family.

ODYSSEUS: the resourceful hero of Homer's *Iliad* and (especially) his *Odyssey*, which tells the stories of his arduous journey home from the Trojan War.

PERDICCAS: this is Perdiccas II, king of Macedon *c.*450–413 BC. He was a great king who succeeded in uniting Macedonia and in weakening the influence of foreign powers on the country. It was his death which sparked the coup of Archelaus (q.v.).

PERICLES: *c.*495–429 BC, an outstanding statesman and the virtual ruler of supposedly democratic Athens from about 450 until his death from the plague. See also notes on 455e, 515e, 516a.

PINDAR: 518–438 BC, from Cynoscephalae. Arguably the greatest of the Greek lyric poets.

PLUTO: also known as Hades or Dis. Brother of Zeus and Poseidon, in a tripartite world he gained the underworld as his domain, while Zeus took the upper air and Poseidon the surface of the earth.

POLUS: from Acragas in Sicily, a pupil of Gorgias, and imitator of his rhetorical techniques. He was the author of a handbook on rhetoric, and a professional teacher of the subject. Plato's portrait of him is severe: he is rude and unintelligent. Callicles' robust self-reliance would almost have seemed attractive to Plato, especially in his youth, if it were not so arrogant; but there is little attractive about Polus' superficial ideas, though Plato may well have taken them to be typical of his times.

POSEIDON: brother of Zeus and Pluto, and lord of the surface of the earth (hence mainly of the sea), as Zeus is of the upper air and Pluto is of the underworld.

PROMETHEUS: his name means 'foresight', which perhaps explains why Zeus used him as he did at 523d–e: since foresight is his domain, he deprived humans of their foreknowledge of their death, so that it always comes as a surprise. More generally, he is seen in Greek myth as a benefactor of humanity, especially by providing them with the civilizing and evolutionary knowledge of fire.

RHADAMANTHYS: brother of Minos (q.v.). Little legend accrued to him, apart from his being just and hence becoming one of the judges in the underworld.

SARAMBUS: an otherwise unknown wine-merchant.

SISYPHUS: one of the great sinners of Greek myth, though details of his crime against Zeus are unclear. His punishment was to roll a stone up a hill, which then rolled back down and he had to start all over again.

TANTALUS: perhaps the most famous of the great sinners of Greek myth. Of the several versions of his story, the best-known has him standing in a pool of water, with a fruit-laden tree above him. Every time he bends down for a drink, the water recedes; every time he reaches up for some food, the branches withdraw. This was punishment to fit the crime, because he had killed and cooked his son Pelops and served him up to the gods to see if they could tell.

TEISANDER: a scarcely known, but wealthy, Athenian of the time.

THEARION: the most famous baker in Athens at the end of the fifth century.

THEMISTOCLES: *c*.530–462 BC. A great Athenian military commander during the Persian Wars, and the statesman chiefly responsible for establishing Athens' potential for greatness after the wars. See also notes on 455e, 517c.

THERSITES: the only non-aristocrat to have a speaking part in Homer's *Iliad* (2. 212 ff.); it is not a favourable part, however, and to later ages he was the archetype of the buffoon or villain.

TITYUS: for attempting to rape the Titan Leto, he was punished in Hades by being spread-eagled on the ground and having vultures rip out his liver (which was seen as the seat of desire). Each night the liver grew again, ready for the vultures the next day.

XERXES: king of Persia 486–465 BC, notorious in Greece for his invasion in 480, which was at first highly successful, but later defeated; the historian Herodotus is our main source. See also note on 483d.

ZETHUS: see Amphion.

ZEUS: chief god of the Olympian pantheon; god of the skies; brother of Pluto and Poseidon.

ZEUXIS: fl. *c*.415 BC. A painter of famously realistic pictures.

The Oxford World's Classics Website

www.worldsclassics.co.uk

- Browse the full range of Oxford World's Classics online

- Sign up for our monthly e-alert to receive information on new titles

- Read extracts from the Introductions

- Listen to our editors and translators talk about the world's greatest literature with our Oxford World's Classics audio guides

- Join the conversation, follow us on Twitter at OWC_Oxford

- Teachers and lecturers can order inspection copies quickly and simply via our website

www.worldsclassics.co.uk

American Literature

British and Irish Literature

Children's Literature

Classics and Ancient Literature

Colonial Literature

Eastern Literature

European Literature

Gothic Literature

History

Medieval Literature

Oxford English Drama

Poetry

Philosophy

Politics

Religion

The Oxford Shakespeare

A complete list of Oxford World's Classics, including Authors in Context, Oxford English Drama, and the Oxford Shakespeare, is available in the UK from the Marketing Services Department, Oxford University Press, Great Clarendon Street, Oxford OX2 6DP, or visit the website at www.oup.com/uk/worldsclassics.

In the USA, visit www.oup.com/us/owc for a complete title list.

Oxford World's Classics are available from all good bookshops. In case of difficulty, customers in the UK should contact Oxford University Press Bookshop, 116 High Street, Oxford OX1 4BR.

	Classical Literary Criticism
	The First Philosophers: The Presocrates and the Sophists
	Greek Lyric Poetry
	Myths from Mesopotamia
APOLLODORUS	**The Library of Greek Mythology**
APOLLONIUS OF RHODES	**Jason and the Golden Fleece**
APULEIUS	**The Golden Ass**
ARISTOPHANES	**Birds and Other Plays**
ARISTOTLE	**The Nicomachean Ethics** **Physics** **Politics**
BOETHIUS	**The Consolation of Philosophy**
CAESAR	**The Civil War** **The Gallic War**
CATULLUS	**The Poems of Catullus**
CICERO	**Defence Speeches** **The Nature of the Gods** **On Obligations** **The Republic** and **The Laws**
EURIPIDES	**Bacchae and Other Plays** **Medea and Other Plays** **Orestes and Other Plays** **The Trojan Women and Other Plays**
GALEN	**Selected Works**
HERODOTUS	**The Histories**
HOMER	**The Iliad** **The Odyssey**